Old & NEW

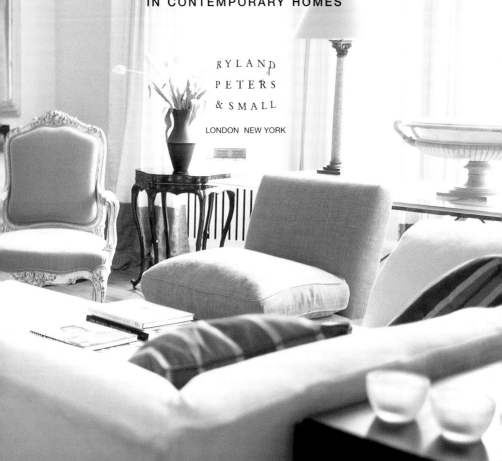

KATHERINE SORRELL

Old & NEW

COMBINING PAST AND PRESENT
IN CONTEMPORARY HOMES

RYLAND
PETERS
& SMALL

LONDON NEW YORK

First published in the USA in 2002
This compact edition published in 2007
by Ryland Peters & Small, Inc.
519 Broadway
5th Floor
New York, NY 10012
www.rylandpeters.com

10 9 8 7 6 5 4 3 2 1

ISBN-10: 1-84597-547-2
ISBN-13: 978-1-84597-547-0

Text copyright © Katherine Sorrell 2002, 2007
Design and photographs copyright
© Ryland Peters & Small 2002, 2007

A CIP record for this book is available from the Library of Congress.

Printed and bound in China.

For this edition:
SENIOR EDITOR Henrietta Heald
DESIGNER Sarah Rock
PICTURE RESEARCH Emily Westlake
PRODUCTION Gemma Moules
PUBLISHING DIRECTOR Alison Starling

CONTENTS

INTRODUCTION

For most of us, decorating is not simply a question of taking an empty room and filling it with brand-new, coordinated furnishings, nor is it a case of inheriting a matching set of priceless antiques. Usually, we're somewhere in the middle—a couple of hand-me-downs here, some chain-store pieces there, a few things found at a secondhand store, maybe a special item we've saved up for. And then, of course, our homes are constantly evolving—things wear out or go out of fashion, we get bored with them, or they're no longer useful. The old-and-new approach to decorating is a realistic way of tackling these challenges, of celebrating the eclectic mix that surrounds us, and of creating a beautiful, comfortable, characterful response.

Combining old and new—whether in a seamless, harmonious blend, or in a dramatic and surprising juxtaposition—can be done in any room in the home. In this book we have chosen the living room, bedroom, kitchen, and bathroom as examples, but there is no reason why you shouldn't extend the principles to a hallway, sunroom, or home office.

Wherever you try this approach, there are endless variations. Your scheme may be based on one precious piece surrounded by relatively neutral furnishings, or it may be more diverse, blending all sorts of items together in an intriguing, eye-catching way; it may contrast period architectural detailing with 21st-century sofas and chairs, or place 18th- and 19th-century antiques in an ultramodern interior; it may take a single color as its starting point, or an ethnic theme, or perhaps retro style. What's for sure, however, is that every scheme will be unique and individual.

There are no hard and fast rules when it comes to mixing old and new, but it's worth following the guidelines given on the following pages and drawing inspiration from the illuminating photographs and detailed text. I hope you find this book exciting and informative, and that it prompts you to be bold, imaginative, and experimental, creating rooms that are as good to be in as they are to look at.

the
spaces

LIVING SPACES

A mix of old and new pieces can create a living room that is both elegant and eclectic. By pairing new furnishings with older pieces that have developed a pleasing patina of age, you can create a balance in which textures, colors, shapes, and styles combine and contrast beautifully, and where subtle harmonies and dramatic differences result in luxurious and relaxing rooms.

THIS PAGE AND OPPOSITE **In this welcoming room, plain walls and a bare wooden floor are offset by luxurious accessories such as velvet-** covered pillows and a satin and mohair throw; the sofa, although it is upholstered in classic leather, has simple contemporary lines.

RELAXED MODERN

Combining old and new results in a wonderful mix of the laidback and the impressive—an interior that is both enjoyable to be in and a pleasure to behold. Introducing antique, retro, or salvaged furnishings into a modern environment instantly tones down any harsh lines, injects a dash of warmth to cool colors, and adds the appealing characteristics of the aged, the worn, and the well-loved. The overall look can be as modern as you like, but adding just one or two old pieces provides the necessary air of easygoing repose and mellow satisfaction.

The starting point for relaxed modern is always a sense of space: a modern aesthetic can never be achieved if there is too much clutter. Airy, light-filled rooms are ideal, but if your living room is dark and poky there are plenty of ways to lighten it up.

Paint the walls a pale, muted color and use light-colored flooring—pale wood, natural matting, or carpet; you could consider pickling or painting dark floorboards. Minimize window treatments, using the simplest of curtains or shades—or perhaps even dispensing with window hangings altogether. Make sure that any unattractive or inessential item is stored out of sight, so that you create as much space as possible and the focus is solely on useful or beautiful objects that you love to have around.

LEFT **A pair of old armchairs have been reupholstered in vintage wool blankets to create an inviting corner for rest and relaxation in a minimalist London loft.**

LEFT, ABOVE **Modern sofas and chairs are counterpointed by a well-worn old cupboard.**
OPPOSITE Classic Le Corbusier **armchairs mingle happily with flea-market pieces.**

OPPOSITE **Limited wooden floorboards and a plain, almost austere backdrop give this London loft a pared-down feel, in spite of its period furniture in worn leather and chintz fabric. The look relies for its effect on lack of clutter and the impact of spots of color in a light-filled room.** BELOW **The neutral hues that distinguish** this flat are calmly contemporary. The mix includes modern suede-covered pouffes, a classic armchair, and, above the radiator, a 1930s Doulton Acid jug. RIGHT **Pieces from very different eras are juxtaposed in this relaxed room. The fireplace has an almost medieval feel, while the chairs are modern, covered in hard-wearing denim.**

Once the bare bones are in place, you can give some thought to your furnishings. The one essential is a capacious couch or, better still, a pair of them. The sofa can be either old or new; if it is old, make sure it doesn't have any uncomfortable broken springs, or worn or torn upholstery. Old sofas, especially in leather, can have a delightfully aged texture, but sometimes recovering, in a hard-wearing plain cotton, velvet, or bouclé, results in an enormous improvement. Again, pale colors (although impractical if you have children or pets) tend to emphasize a modern aesthetic. You might prefer a couple of armchairs that are large enough to curl up in, or even a chaise longue, which will inevitably add a note of languid elegance to the most pared-down of interiors.

Whatever the size of your living space, an abundance of storage is important, so you may find that an antique chest or armoire or an old cabinet or sideboard makes a useful addition to the mix. A blanket chest or footlooker, for example,

makes a superb contrast with minimal, modern furnishings, while a lean, low 1950s sideboard would ideally complement their sleek lines and slim styling. Or, for an impressive focal point and a distinct change of tone, opt for a more decorative piece such as an old English hutch with distressed paintwork or an antique French armoire with carved detailing.

When you are buying old or antique furniture, look out for well-made pieces in good-quality materials and simple, understated colors. Natural materials have their own innate integrity, so are always superior to synthetic ones. In a living room, the seductive textures of heavy grained wood, cool stone, patinated leather, and crisp cotton or linen will combine to create a reassuringly timeless atmosphere. Teaming these materials with shades of white, cream, taupe, stone, and gray makes for relaxing surroundings, although it's important to include occasional splashes of color—perhaps some old chintz made into pillow covers, a vintage Welsh blanket used as a sofa throw, some smoky 1970s glassware, or a bold 1950s block-print poster. In general, it is advisable to limit the number of accessories, but displaying one or two carefully chosen pieces that express your interests or

ABOVE The eclectic pieces in this airy Paris apartment, dating from several different periods, all share a clarity of line and feel of skilled craftsmanship which means that they look just right together.
LEFT If you discover a tacky old sofa in a secondhand store, you could take inspiration from the owners of this Dutch home and simply swathe it in cream linen or cotton sheets, tucking them in around the edges. The wrinkles and creases contribute to the easygoing, laidback look.

personality, whether they be centuries old or made a few years ago, will result in an appealing effect and an entirely contemporary feel.

Last, but not least, think about how lighting can alter the feel of your living room. Discreet low-voltage downlighters set into the ceiling are almost invisible, but they cast enough light for reading or writing and to showcase prized ornaments and pictures. They can be supplemented with attractive period fixtures that possess more character, such as a classic gooseneck lamp or a simple Victorian-style silk shade, perhaps with beading around the edge. And don't forget that the soft, flickering glow cast by candlelight is the most restful and flattering illumination of all.

When putting together a relaxed contemporary look, it is essential to balance elements that will have a softening and soothing effect with those that are more formal and structured. With the right choices of old and new, your living room will gain character from an enviable mix: the grace of the past with the sophistication of the present.

ABOVE The tranquil atmosphere in this converted church derives from the warm colors of the wooden floor and furniture, and the restful simplicity of the repeated motif of horizontal and vertical lines. Old church chairs sit beside a modern daybed and a robust retro coffee table with chrome legs. RIGHT Several rugs, a country-style dining table and chairs, and a classic gooseneck lamp soften the industrial ethos of this extension to a converted gasworks.

LEFT **The textural contrast of faux fur adds glamour to a classic armchair.**
LEFT, BELOW **A touch of gold, in the form of an 18th-century French chair, livens up a muted palette.**
RIGHT **A Georgian-style sofa has been plainly upholstered so as not to detract from the elaborately framed mirror. A mid-20th-century chair adds another point of interest**
OPPOSITE **The floor and walls make a neutral backdrop for a strong theme of blue and gold.**

GOLD & GLAMOUR

Whether the aim is to create an interior with plenty of impact or to achieve a feel of subtle luxury, nothing beats the glamour of gold. In small quantities, gold adds understated elegance; in larger quantities, it brings high-voltage opulence and drama.

You need only one splash of gold to make this style work, giving your living room a bold focal point while the rest of the furnishings are quietly complementary. For an eye-catching look, choose a piece that is oversized and ornate. An enormous gilt-framed mirror, for example, could be propped against a white wall for a vivid contrast in color and texture. To show the piece off to best effect, keep the decorative theme simple—painted floorboards rather than thick carpets; Roman shades rather than dressy swagged curtains.

If your style isn't quite so minimal, it's possible to mix and match a few pieces that share similar attributes—a curving gilt-legged table, for example, will sit happily alongside another item that has the same

THIS PAGE Curving shapes are a subtly repeated motif in this sitting room. Muted colors and the absence of pattern promote harmony between disparate pieces of furniture.

FAR LEFT The velvet-covered French Art Deco armchairs have a sumptuous feel that complements the lines of the modern coffee table. LEFT An antique candelabra fills an empty fireplace to dramatic effect. BELOW An all-white room provides an excellent backdrop for glamour. Just add a single oversized, eye-catching piece such as this carved antique gilt mirror.

attention-grabbing qualities, such as curvaceous Murano glass or an elaborate antique chandelier. Take care not to go overboard, or the effect could become clumsy rather than covetable.

For a more subtle look, combine textures and colors that give an impression of understated luxury. Choose fabrics such as velvet, silk, faux fur, and metallic organza, and shapes that twist and twine in an intricate fashion. Elaborate carving, in small doses, enhances this look, particularly when contrasted with relatively minimal surroundings. Decorative elements such as beading, fringing, patterned rugs, and Venetian glass mirrors have a similar effect. Splashes of deep, rich color—berry reds, midnight blues, or chocolate browns—against a pale background will create an atmosphere of indulgence. Clever touches such as these need not cost a fortune, but will come together to create a living room that possesses dreamy, divine glamour in endless abundance.

ABOVE The bare white walls, exposed brickwork, and white vinyl floor give this loft an industrial aesthetic. But it is furnished almost entirely with mid-20th-century pieces, from the plywood Eames chair of 1946 in the foreground to the 1960s Castigioni-inspired floor lamp. The seating on the left is also 1960s in flavor, while the sideboard and sunburst clock are characteristic of the 1950s. The eclectic mixture is both fresh and appealing.

ABOVE LEFT Its plain, flat front and tapering splayed legs put this sideboard firmly in the 1950s. Objects on display are mid-century, too, but the overall feel is more modern, thanks to the prints on the wall above and the vinyl flooring.

LEFT Although this 1950s sofa is minimal enough to pass as modern, the two table lamps that flank it are very much of their time.

RETRO-INSPIRED

Furniture and accessories produced in the mid-20th century have a distinctive energy and optimism all of their own. Such pieces, whether celebrated modern classics or unassuming pieces by an anonymous designer, have become increasingly popular in contemporary homes, complementing modern schemes in a manner that is attractive, easygoing, and full of character.

Mid-century retro style can encompass designs from the 1930s through to the 1970s, but, for a fresh, simple look that is not difficult to put together, seek out pieces from the 1950s and early 1960s. Sofas, chairs, and sideboards from this era are slimline and clean-cut, often raised off the floor on spindly, splayed legs; colors are fresh and clear; and accessories such as clocks, vases, and lamps tend toward the quirky and eye-catching.

To create a retro-inspired living room requires only one key piece, though many people find that once they have bought one item they

LEFT The traditional character of an old wood-burning stove contrasts with a pair of burnt-orange armchairs by British designer Robin Day. This room is mostly furnished with lucky secondhand finds. RIGHT A double-height ceiling and an expanse of plain white walls in this converted office building on the outskirts of Paris allow a pair of retro-style armchairs, recovered in navy velvet, to flaunt their shapely forms.

become fascinated with the period and simply cannot stop. A long, lean sofa is a good start—either an expensive version by a well-known designer such as Florence Knoll, a re-edition by a major manufacturer, or a lucky secondhand find that needs reupholstering. Integrate this into a contemporary room by keeping the surroundings as plain as possible—bare boards, parquet, or rush matting are best for floors, while white-painted walls allow the distinctive silhouettes of these pieces to stand out. Sideboards and armchairs from the period are key pieces, too, as are spindly lamps with conical shades. If your living room is large enough to incorporate a dining table, you could offset it with a set of typically 1950s Scandinavian chairs.

Retro pieces will integrate well with modern furnishings in a 21st-century living room, thanks to their pared-down, delicate designs. They can also make fabulous statements in period homes, standing out against molding, ceiling details, and paneling as unexpected contrasts. More eccentric accessories, used with care, introduce splashes of color and fun. After all, this is a look that doesn't take itself too seriously, but creates a combination of old and new that is fresh, individual, and thoroughly enjoyable to live with.

GLOBAL FUSION

In the same way that combining old and new sets up exciting harmonies and contrasts, mixing pieces from East and West creates similarly intriguing juxtapositions. Whether you introduce modern Chinese-style seating into a period living room, or make ancient Oriental artifacts the focal point of a contemporary loft space, a fusion of global styles from a variety of periods is a unique way to bring character and interest to any home.

This look works best when the decorative scheme is based on intense colors such as crimson, chocolate, or indigo, which have the ability to transform a living space into an inviting cocoon. If you prefer a lighter look, simply use a single element of dramatic color combined with white, taupe, gray, or another neutral shade.

In many Eastern cultures, homes tend to be furnished far more sparsely than in the West and to feature seating that is close to the ground. By

ABOVE AND OPPOSITE **This distinctive modern home in Yorkshire was converted from a chapel dating from 1834. The building retains its original stone pillars and wooden floor. The modern, Oriental-style furniture (above) seems initially to create a** stark contrast, but in fact its simple, angular lines perfectly complement those of the old building. The result is a calm, peaceful space that has been given an injection of warmth and drama by the vivid red cushions that top the chairs and the benches.

removing extraneous furnishings and accessories and choosing low-level seating, you will instantly make a start toward creating a distinctly global look. For impact, choose furniture with strong forms or ethnic designs—an Oriental-style chair with a solid, square shape, perhaps, or an African "throne." Either would make a striking contrast with European furniture from any era. Dark woods, cane, and brass are all typical materials, and very different from 21st-century pine, concrete, and stainless steel.

An African sculpture or woven basket, Indian saris made into pillow covers, an antique Turkish kilim used as a wall-hanging—these and similar items can all can be used to introduce an element of the exotic into an interior. When aiming to create a pared-down, zenlike feel in a room, use just one or two favorite pieces; for a more dramatic, opulent, and embellished style, combine items old and new from around the globe and create an intriguing interior that has immediate warmth and unabashed personality.

LEFT AND FAR LEFT This tranquil living room is decorated in predominantly neutral tones, with two red-painted walls that add vibrancy. The furniture combines new and old, East and West, with simple, spare shapes sitting side by side in a seamless mix. BELOW LEFT Its simple sculptural shape, thrown into relief by the antique wooden screen, imparts an Oriental flavor to this modern vase. RIGHT Red-painted beams create an Oriental feel in a very old Paris apartment. The modern modular sofa is complemented by an antique rustic chair and coffee table. A hard floor inset with an intriguing pattern of octagonal tiles completes the mix.

LIVING SPACES: getting it right

• Keep it simple—don't try to cram too much furniture into a living room. When mixing pieces from different periods, you need only a few examples of each.

• When you have one very strong pattern in a room, aim to keep the rest of the furnishings plain, avoiding clashes and allowing the pattern the chance to make a dramatic statement.

• For the lines of furniture to stand out properly, wall treatments should be pale and understated.

• Old chairs, from any era, look great reupholstered in white or off-white fabric. Alternatively, have slipcovers made, for a more informal look.

• Lengths of old fabric can be made into pillow covers. Against a plain backdrop, florals, toiles, and 1960s prints look marvelous, adding plenty of character and color.

• For old pieces to work with new ones, they should have a similar feel. Choose clean-lined, pared-down items, and look for shapes that echo each other, such as gently curving lines or boxy silhouettes.

• Look for good-quality furniture that has a timeless style. Excellence in design, a high standard of craftsmanship, and solid, natural materials provide common factors that unify different pieces, whatever their age.

• Use color to coordinate. For example, if a piece of wooden furniture is out of harmony with the other elements of your living room, try painting it the same color as the walls.

• Remember that scale is important. One overscaled piece will make an impact, but avoid mixing lots of large and small pieces in one room, or the effect will be crowded and cluttered.

• Attention to scale is also important when it comes to the details. If a table is average in size but has heavy, square legs, for example, it will look wrong next to a chair of similar proportions with slender, tapering legs.

• To avoid creating visual confusion, keep accessories to a minimum, choosing a few low-key, timeless pieces or just a single bold item.

THIS PAGE **Surprising combinations and bold contrasts work well in kitchens. Here, the warmth of old wood offsets the glossy sheen of a stainless-steel pan.**
RIGHT **In perfect condition, dining chairs dating from the 1950s (including a fine set of Cherner dining chairs by Norman Cherner) are grouped around a matching table. Their curving lines and warm tones contrast with a shiny modern work unit.**

COOKING & EATING SPACES

The kitchen and dining room offer ample opportunities for pairing the traditional with the contemporary. Modern appliances look good contrasted with old-fashioned implements, while new dining tables can be mixed with old chairs, and fitted units can be offset by quirky period pieces.

OPPOSITE, ABOVE A quirky mix of old and new is emphasized by dramatic lighting. OPPOSITE, BELOW The lamps, bowl and minimal blind add an unobtrusive modern twist to a dining room with a beautiful original parquet floor. LEFT Rough brick walls inset with wooden beams make a contrasting backdrop to a stylish contemporary dining table and chairs. RIGHT Plain white walls and a grid of black-and-white photographs add chic modernity to a kitchen made from reclaimed timber.

URBAN SOPHISTICATION

Whether you live in a 21st-century loft, a Federal townhouse, or an Arts and Crafts apartment, a casual mix of old and new is an ideal way to soften the hard edges of city living, bringing uncontrived warmth and individuality to an urban dining room or kitchen. Using contemporary furnishings and smart detailing makes it easy to create a sophisticated room that looks impressive and effective, but adding older materials, furniture, and accessories will bring the space to life.

The key to this look is texture—every bit as essential an element as color and form. Contrasting textures can be understated or dramatic, but are always satisfying, bringing an indefinable pleasure and sense of satisfaction to the look and feel of a room. To combine textures requires some careful consideration, but is not excessively difficult. Balance hard against soft, pitted against smooth, matte

LEFT Classic Arne Jacobsen dining chairs, with wooden frames and slender steel legs, harmonize perfectly with the modern, clean-lined wood and metal dining table.
RIGHT AND OPPOSITE Handy open shelving and displays of stylish accessories and foodstuffs help to soften the sleek modernity of angular fitted units.

against shiny, and the result will be enjoyable and enriching. When using old and new, this comes completely naturally: rugged brick walls against fabric-covered dining chairs; sleek stainless-steel countertops against rough plasterwork; a grainy wood dining table with a plastic hanging lamp.

High-quality materials and workmanship are essential for a chic city kitchen or dining room. Rustic finishes won't do; instead, tables, chairs, cabinets, and surfaces should be sleek and well turned out, functional but also beautiful. If you are teaming a set of 1950s dining chairs with a new table, for example, ensure that each has its own integrity of form, so that the two looks don't clash.

Finally, add a variety of accessories, perhaps an old industrial-style lamp hanging low over the table, a French enamel sign on the wall, a few contemporary photographs in symmetrical rows, or simply a trio of clear glass vases—finishing touches that encapsulate the subtle yet carefully thought-out combinations that make this look so attractive.

LEFT Lots of light and a spacious layout give this kitchen a modern feel, emphasized by the cream built-in units. Traditional elements include a woodworking bench, a set of old weighing scales, and high stools. ABOVE Even with new built-in units, this kitchen has a rural feel, thanks to the traditional checkerboard floor tiles and the unusual swan-necked faucet.

TOP The timeless quality of this wood-veneer wall treatment is offset by traditional faucets, a 1930s clip-on spotlight and an array of good-looking kitchen equipment. ABOVE RIGHT The scrubbed wooden floorboards, old-fashioned fridge, and freestanding furniture contrast with the white-on-white color scheme, which gives a minimal-meets-rural effect.

CONTEMPORARY COUNTRY

A kitchen decorated in country fashion does not have to be traditional or twee. Putting a more contemporary spin on country decor creates an interior that still possesses all the ease and relaxation that makes the country look so appealing, but with a fresh, modern edge that is a delight to live with.

The important thing to remember about the modern country kitchen is that it shouldn't look too "fitted." Naturally, you need plenty of storage and workspace, but that doesn't mean bland, square units and laminated counters. Instead, mix modern, built-in elements with an old hutch or butcher's block, a freestanding side table with a low shelf underneath, or simply rows of open shelving.

Some materials are more suitable than others. Knotty pine, for example, tends to look dated and cottagelike, although other good-quality woods have a lovely appearance that softens and warms a room. Painted wood gives a country feel without being old-fashioned,

RIGHT Even in a kitchen with modern built-in units, you can create a rural effect. Simply add open shelving for the display of kettles, teapots, or other items, poles or hooks from which to hang saucepans and general implements, and a large table flanked by a set of mismatched chairs. BELOW This kitchen features capacious storage cupboards with roomy drawers beneath to contain clutter. A comfortably large dining table, in sturdy, plain, country style, is matched by a set of simple wooden chairs. The bold contemporary print on the wall counterpoints the other decorative elements in terms of color and style. OPPOSITE Built-in and freestanding items happily coexist in this yellow-themed kitchen, and tidy rows of stainless-steel canisters contrast with the rough surface of an old dining table.

and is an excellent way of disguising any less-than-perfect pieces. Stripped original wooden boards are the ideal flooring, while ceramic tiles are the most practical solution for the walls above sinks or countertops. Touches of cane and metal are useful additions to the textural mix.

Overall, aim to achieve a feeling of light and space. Hang Roman shades or sheer voile at the windows to allow in plenty of sunlight, and keep walls and floors plain. Furniture, although sturdy, should be simple, and accessories kept to a minimum, so that each piece creates impact rather than getting lost in clutter. Glass-fronted cabinets are better than ones with solid panels for adding to the open, airy feel. Finally, keep displays on the formal side. If you have open shelves, it takes discipline to maintain a tidy appearance, but well-spaced rows of pans, boxes, or ornaments demonstrate an easygoing country aesthetic combined with a more considered modern style.

OPPOSITE There is a lovely balance here between old wood and steel. The white tiles, while subtle, link the two materials. LEFT Upholstered chairs offset the straight lines and hard metal of a high-tech kitchen. BELOW Although they don't match, these old and new freestanding units possess the same good-looking and hard-working qualities.

WOOD AND STEEL

A combination of wood and steel almost invariably looks good, the gleaming, reflective nature of metal providing an ideal foil to the more traditional elegance of grained wood. It is a mix that works particularly well in a kitchen, where the necessity for lots of hard, rectangular planes means that it can be all too easy to suffer from monotonous surface textures. The addition of a contrasting material makes all the difference, creating interest, personality, and sophisticated appeal.

There are plenty of ways in which to combine wood and steel, the simplest of all being to add wooden chairs to a stainless-steel kitchen, or vice versa. This will soften the ambience of a kitchen made entirely from one material, making it both more visually exciting and more comfortable to live with. Equally simple would be to add stainless-steel handles or solid-wood knobs. Alternatively, you could add metal appliances and accessories—refrigerators, dishwashers, even toasters or lemon squeezers.

GLORIOUS COLOR

It is all too easy to see antiques as no more than pieces of boring brown furniture. But there is a wealth of ways in which to inject luscious color by using a mix of old and new. Kitchens are ideal for this treatment. In living rooms, bedrooms, and bathrooms you may want calm, glamour, or relaxation, but in the kitchen you can afford a little over-the-top exuberance and uninhibited fun.

Going global is one means of interpreting this look, choosing a fusion of ethnic pieces to create a fun and funky feel. One item may provide a focal point, such as a Moroccan star lantern, a painted Oriental screen, or a Gujerati embroidered door-hanging. Or you may prefer to combine a host of items from around the world—Chinese silk tea cozies, Mexican glassware, salvaged French blue-and-white tiles—for an eclectic mix that is rich, exotic, and unusual.

Another option is to find retro-style pieces in vivid, unsubtle colorways, from Jacobsenesque dining chairs in bubblegum pink to

FAR LEFT, ABOVE AND BELOW The blue-and-white tiles make a marvelous backdrop to a set of patterned ceramic containers and a modern (albeit classically detailed) stove. The marble-topped breakfast table is an antique find, while the pink chair is a modern re-edition of a classic Arne Jacobsen design. Overall, the look is feminine and light, but the room is practical as well as good-looking.

LEFT AND RIGHT A modern cooker is an efficient addition to a global-style kitchen. The star lantern and turquoise tiles make allusions to Moorish style but the eclectic theme incorporates items as diverse as silk tea cosies from China and doorknobs from India and Africa.

OPPOSITE **Cobalt-blue woodwork and yellow walls set off the table, chairs, cupboard, and filing cabinet, all in distressed wood, but the most eye-catching element is the dishes—a mix of handmade items by distinguished ceramicist Rupert Spira and cheap chain-store pieces.**

LEFT, ABOVE **A collection of old Indian lassi cups makes an unusual display as well as providing storage for kitchen utensils.**
LEFT, BELOW **The sink and faucet were both found in salvage yards; their utilitarian looks make a good foil for a child's painting and kitsch ceramics.**

BELOW **Oriental style meets the 1950s in this dining area. The chairs and table have the typical splayed, tapering legs of 1950s design, while the coolie shade of the lamp on the right, combined with the antique screen and chest, introduces a Chinese note to this quirky mix.**

food containers in pretty pastels. Alternatively, simply choose contemporary items, from table linen to china, from tiles to lighting, that feature bold, bright shades, mixing them with old tables, chairs, and cupboards. If all else fails, you can always add some intensely colored bowls and plates, a vivid freestanding lamp, or some homemade artwork, and paint bland built-in units in strong, attractive tones.

MID-CENTURY MODERN

LEFT In this open-plan 1970s house, the dining table and chairs, 1950s designs by Charles and Ray Eames, double as a work space. Their metal and plastic finish harmonizes with the modern white kitchen, while the wooden floor, bare window and few accessories are perfectly in tune with the look.
ABOVE This 1960s penthouse flat was refitted in the 1990s. The kitchen itself couldn't be more modern, with plain white and glass-fronted units and stainless steel. The Tulip dining suite, however, is by Eero Saarinen and dates from 1957; although the table's teak top and the chocolate-colored corduroy chair seats are firmly of their time, the juxtaposition is harmonious.

There is something very distinctive about the furniture designed in the middle years of the 20th century. Not only is it characterized by classic good looks and timeless appeal, but also it combines effortlessly with modern architecture and furnishings, never looking frumpy or outdated but always fresh and inspiring. A marvelous place to incorporate such mid-century designer pieces in your home is in the kitchen or dining area.

Unfortunately, it is no longer at all likely that you will come across such pieces by chance in yard sales, dumpsters or house clearances. The popularity of mid-century furniture means that prices are high, but you can still source it through specialized dealers or at auctions. Alternatively, several firms still continue to manufacture pieces to the original designs, while others produce close copies that, to the non-purist, are just as attractive.

To make sure this particular combination of old and new really looks at its best, you need to start by getting rid of clutter and

reducing accessories to a minimum. The lines of mid-century furniture pieces are pure and pared down, and to be appreciated at their best they need to be seen without unnecessary distraction.

Walls that are painted white, off-white, taupe, stone, or beige provide a subtle background, as do unadorned wooden floors and windows. The square, regular shapes of a contemporary kitchen make a perfect complement to mid-century furniture, particularly if you pay attention to details such as handles and faucets.

Lighting should be similarly well thought out; modern recessed spotlights are ideally suited to this sort of decorative scheme, in that they throw light precisely where it is required without drawing attention to themselves. Alternatively, a simple

shade, either antique or modern, can work well when hung low over a dining table.

Even the most minimal and high tech of contemporary kitchens can look wonderful when mixed with mid-century furnishings—sleek stainless-steel or lacquered white units combine beautifully with curving plastic, wood or metal. Steer clear of paneled cupboards with fussy detailing or anything that looks remotely rustic— this is a forward-looking, urban style. Accessories, too, such as storage jars, pots and pans, utensils and gadgets, should be selected for their clean lines and clarity of form, in materials such as stainless steel, glass, and chrome. If anything hits the wrong note, the solution is simple—hide it in a cupboard and firmly close the door.

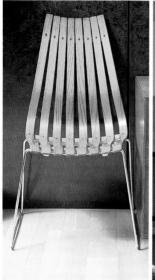

ABOVE AND OPPOSITE, LEFT A built-in kitchen in glossy white and stainless steel is home to an array of classic gadgets and some unusual retro-style chairs. OPPOSITE, RIGHT Norman Cherner designed these Cherner chairs in 1958. Grouped around a matching dining table, they make a striking centerpiece in an up-to-date kitchen with wooden floors and a stainless-steel splashback. RIGHT A Noguchi paper lantern sails above a table with integrated candle holders, designed by an architectural practice called The Moderns. The plywood and metal Arne Jacobsen chairs complement the materials used in other parts of the room.

COOKING & EATING SPACES: getting it right

• Combine and contrast textures for a feel that is inviting and individual: smooth, shiny stainless steel against rough, bare brickwork, or grained wood against soft cotton upholstery, for example.

• Aim to provide plenty of storage—but not necessarily in the form of built-in modern units. Old hutches, cupboards, butchers' blocks, and open shelves are all great additions to the mix.

• Choose efficient modern appliances—dishwashers, stoves, exhaust fans, and so on—and mix them with older accessories, or hide them behind specially made cabinet doors.

• The heights of old and new chairs and dining tables may not match up, so take measurements carefully before you rush into making a purchase.

• Create straightforward contrasts between old and new by choosing objects that are well defined and simple in style. If a piece combines more than one style in itself, it will create visual clutter and detract from the overall look.

• Modern kitchens tend to be very square and hard-edged. If this look doesn't suit you, add furniture with curvy outlines (such as old Paris café chairs) or items that are softer and more giving—perhaps an antique Turkish kilim under a dining table, or a pair of pretty 1950s curtains.

• Be disciplined about open shelves and work surfaces. Having many small items on display is never as effective as a few carefully chosen pieces. One huge antique wooden bowl full of fruit will have much more impact than lots of smaller pieces.

• Old cabinets and hutches can sometimes be massively improved by changing the knobs or handles, or by replacing cracked or warped door panels with fabric, chicken wire, or sandblasted or etched glass.

• Plenty of companies now specialize in modern accessories in classic retro designs—juicers, blenders, and toasters, to name but a few. Use these to inject instant old-and-new style.

• Keep walls and floors plain, and minimize clutter, so that both antique and modern pieces—such as an English oak dining table combined with a set of 1950s Scandinavian chairs —are shown at their best.

SLEEPING SPACES

The bedroom is a private space where you can be decoratively creative. It's the perfect home for your treasured old and new pieces, but for harmony's sake keep things plain and unassuming, and restrict yourself to one or two dramatic flourishes. Don't cram accessories into the room—clutter is neither restful nor relaxing.

THIS PAGE AND OPPOSITE **Sheer** curtains of a loose metallic weave diffuse natural light as it falls upon a disparate but harmonious collection of pieces The antique mahogany bed, set off by pale lilac walls, highlights the very different texture and color of a sleek white-leather Mies van der Rohe chair. But the two items share a curvaceous opulence that is set off by the luxurious fur throw and rug.

FAR LEFT Layers of white bed linen adorn an old iron bed with pretty detailing. The effect is spare and utilitarian but ultimately calming. LEFT In another plain and simple bedroom, an old chair sits next to a divan, acting as a bedside table. The white bed linen emphasizes the pared-down purity of the space.

PURE & SIMPLE

If you want a bedroom that is a relaxed, calming space in which to refresh the senses, you need to start by creating an atmosphere of tranquil simplicity. Fundamental to this effect is a room that is airy rather than cramped, spacious rather than cluttered. Even in the smallest of bedrooms you can achieve this by putting any inessential items out of sight, leaving only the key pieces: a bed, a side table, a lamp, a mirror, a closet, perhaps a chair, and one or two accessories. A plain floor is best, either scrubbed wood, natural matting, or plain carpet with, if necessary, a single rug beside the bed. Walls, too, should be plain and pale, enhancing the sense of space and light. A painting or two will introduce a personal touch, but try to avoid garish colors and heavy frames.

The key item in any sleeping space is, of course, the bed. A modern divan is nicely understated and many have the benefit of a large storage drawer underneath; an antique bed will be prettier, if perhaps not quite so practical. Victorian iron beds, for example, are lovely, and provide a welcome note of decorative detail in a room that is very pared down. The other essentials for bedroom comfort are textiles. Try not to obscure light at the windows, keeping window

LEFT This plain modern divan is adorned with an antique American patchwork quilt in muted pinks. Next to the bed, two old trunks take the place of a bedside table. On the wall above the bed, a modern painting by American artist Peter Zangrillo acts as an unusual headboard. ABOVE An efficient lamp is essential for anyone who likes reading in bed. This antique hinged-arm version is beautifully simple yet functional.

BELOW When using a mixture of patterns in this type of scheme, make sure they are minimal in style. Basic striped mattress tickings are ideal. RIGHT A collection of black-and-white family photos are hung on a clothesline, and look all the better for this unpretentious treatment. OPPOSITE A four-poster does not have to be an imposing affair. This one has been made from scaffolding poles, making an industrial contrast to the chintz bedspread.

treatments as simple as possible and avoiding fussy pleating and draping, valances and tiebacks. Voile makes gorgeous, inexpensive curtains, while cotton (perhaps with a very small pattern) or ticking can be transformed into a pair of simple gathered drapes. Wooden colonial-style shutters or a wooden venetian blind are two alternatives.

On the bed, choose white bed linen with the most delicate of trimmings. Then either layer white on white with duvet covers, blankets, and throws, or seek antique textiles that have subtle patterning, either patchwork quilts, satin-edged blankets, floral bedcovers, or crochet throws. Make sure there is a simple but practical bedside table to hold a book, a clock, and a small vase of flowers. The finishing touches are a directional bedside lamp and dimmable general lighting to create a soft and restful atmosphere.

ULTRAFEMININE BEDROOMS

LEFT The grandeur of this antique French bed is offset by plain walls and extra-wide wooden floorboards. The feeling of luxury is enhanced by soft pashmina throws and colored lampshades. ABOVE Vintage florals represent the ultimate in femininity. You can use them as the basis for a simple and pretty guest bedroom. In this example, a dark wooden bedstead has been painted a chalky white and teamed with a chintz bedspread. An armful of hydrangeas in an old enamel bucket adds an attractive finishing touch.

Interior fashions may be becoming more modern and minimal, pared down and practical, but there will always be a part of most women that cannot resist the opulence of an ultrafeminine bedroom. This is a real boudoir, a sanctuary offering escape from the stresses and realities of the outside world, a haven that possesses comfort and glamour in equal measure. Old and new combine perfectly in this type of bedroom. It is, for example, the ideal setting for a magnificent antique bed, a one-off investment buy that makes a bold statement and captivates the eye. Whether it is a four-poster, an old metal bed, or a bed made from intricately carved or prettily painted wood, it is crucial that it has a sumptuous, indulgent feel. Add an old chaise longue, an oversized mirror, or a French armoire—any of these pieces will contribute to an evocative, romantic atmosphere.

The other major consideration in a boudoir bedroom is the use of textiles. Even a relatively plain bedroom can be transformed by floral

RIGHT, TOP **This unusual antique bed takes pride of place in a modern room, its opulence highlighted by plain white bed linen. It is paired with an antique ottoman and dressing table, the latter topped by a Venetian-glass mirror. A shocking-pink Indian shawl injects a hot splash.**
RIGHT, MIDDLE **An elegant chaise longue is topped by velvet cushions and a gold sari with metallic-thread embroidery, suggesting the ultimate in sensuality and glamour.**
RIGHT, BOTTOM **Piles of plump antique quilts and bedcovers are a pretty addition to this look.**
OPPOSITE **A carved wooden four-poster dominates a simple bedroom with roughly plastered walls and a wooden floor. The bed is clearly the room's focal point, and the other furnishings are deliberately understated to show it off at its best.**

fabrics or plenty of patchwork quilts or pashmina throws. The key is not to be restrained: you need layer upon cozy layer to make the room really look the part. Choose pinks, lilacs, soft blues, and glamorous golds and bronzes, and remember that texture is important, too—pair shiny Chinese silks with embroidered and beaded Indian pieces and soft, fluffy cashmere, keeping an eye open in antique stores for vintage pieces that can be adapted as throws or pillow covers.

To complete the look, display a generous abundance of accessories. Pile patterned cushions on top of one another. Layer quilts, throws, and bedcovers on the ends of beds, even when the beds are not in use. Either hang pretty pictures and ornate mirrors on the walls or prop them on the floor; and, finally, heap an abundance of flowers in a large container so that their heady scent floats through the room.

LEFT AND OPPOSITE The undulating form of an elegant, curving screen is echoed by that of a modern chaise longue. Paneled walls and a rug add to the feeling of refined luxury.

BELOW In this masculine room, a carefully contrived color scheme pulls together old (a Bertoia Diamond chair dating from 1952) and new (a Richard Sapper Tizio lamp).

UNDERSTATED ELEGANCE

To enjoy a good night's sleep, we need a comfortable bed and calm surroundings—a muted color scheme, simple furniture, subtle lighting. All these elements add up to a bedroom that is sophisticated and elegant, where antiques are combined with chic modern pieces to create an atmosphere that promotes rest and relaxation.

If you want to achieve a look of understated elegance, don't emphasize a single exotic item but try to create a natural combination of furniture and accessories that blend into a seamless whole. The bed itself can be relatively ordinary—a divan is fine—but should be dressed in attractive linens with a smart, tailored appearance. Avoid fuss or frills of any kind, and instead think Brooks Brothers suiting, with narrowly striped or hemstitched sheets.

Enhance the sense of luxury by covering the floor with deep-pile rugs, perhaps with a subtle pattern; you could even hang a rug on the wall for a rich and sumptuous effect—or walls could be paneled

with wood veneer like an upscale gentlemen's club. In general, furnishings should be kept to a minimum, each piece chosen for its quality of materials and manufacture. Secondhand finds are unlikely to make the grade, but classic designer pieces are perfect, with the emphasis on function as well as aesthetics. A bedside table, a chair or a chaise longue, and perhaps a screen to disguise a dressing area, are all that is required—they could be old or new, American, European, or Far Eastern, as long as they demonstrate fine forms and good workmanship.

Lighting is vital to achieving success with this look. Recessed downlighters fitted in the ceiling will give general illumination without unwanted glare or dazzle, while for reading in bed a pair of adjustable

lamps is best—either adjusted to an appropriate height on bedside tables or attached to the wall behind and to either side of the bed. Modern lamps are ideal for this purpose, and have the sort of sleek, slimline design that is appropriate to this understated scheme.

Perhaps the most important consideration of all, however, is color. Avoid bright hues and choose instead naturals and neutrals: white, taupe, ivory, stone, shell, and so on—all of which will enhance the sense of space and light, and result in a calm, considered atmosphere. For a more masculine approach, choose shades of gray, from dove to charcoal, and navy, or even deep reds and greens, resulting in a warm and intimate space that is nevertheless refined, dignified, and tasteful.

SLEEPING SPACES: getting it right

• Avoid bedroom clutter by investing in large closets, armoires, and chests of drawers. These could be modern, built-in versions, with invisible push-touch hinges, or antique versions for a more dramatic and individual statement.

• The bed should be the focal point of the room. If you can afford a beautiful antique, keep the linen simple and understated, so the bed's design can stand out. If you have a modern divan, layer quilts, throws, and pillows for a luxurious effect.

• Clever color schemes can pull a look together, uniting antique and modern pieces. Generally, pale colors such as ivory and taupe are calming and restful, but stronger colors can sometimes be more cozy and inviting. If you have a wonderful bed, you could paint only the wall behind the bed to draw attention to it.

• Keep flooring neutral to provide a plain backdrop that will show off pieces of furniture with interesting shapes and colors to their best advantage.

• A bedside rug is very comforting underfoot. Choose one that's plain or features a subtle pattern that doesn't detract from other furnishings.

• Even if you invest in an antique bed, you should always buy a good-quality new mattress. We spend an average of twenty-five years of our lives in bed, so it's worth making sure your bed is not lumpy, too hard, or too soft.

• Choose furniture linked by color, shape or material. The less fussy the decoration and the cleaner the lines, the more likely that old and new pieces will harmonize well.

• Dimmable lights are a good idea for overall illumination. Recessed downlighters in the ceiling will work with an old-and-new scheme because they don't draw any attention to themselves.

• Accessories can add pretty touches to a bedroom scheme, from enamel pitchers to chintz-printed bowls, from an old sari used as a bedcover to a Venetian-glass mirror, from an African stool to a tailor's dummy.

• Whether it's a sleek, modern halogen light or a 1930s chrome version, an adjustable bedside lamp is indispensable for easy bedtime reading.

BATHING SPACES

A bathroom should be an oasis—an intimate place for contemplation, pampering, and relaxation. Here, a combination of old and new gives a sense of luxury and individuality that will prove the source of endless pleasure. Surprising juxtapositions such as 21st-century faucets paired with a 19th-century roll-top bath create a sense of drama, while subtler details provide food for thought and a chance to unwind in idyllic surroundings.

THIS PAGE AND OPPOSITE The sharp, square outline of this huge bathtub, covered in mosaic tiles (in an appropriate shade of turquoise), is very modern. The effect is tempered by the addition of a pair of antique cross-head faucets, and in the background a cast-iron column radiator. The gently worn patina of these old pieces softens the room and enriches it with a sense of timeless comfort.

LEFT AND OPPOSITE An old roll-top bathtub contrasts with avant-garde Philippe Starck faucets and a sink with an exposed chrome drain.
RIGHT The pair of carvings placed symmetrically in a triangular chimney breast are the focal point of this fashion designer's bathroom.
BELOW RIGHT This bath is simply a rectangular box sunk deep into the floor of an intimate side room. Tiny mosaic tiles and a stone wall provide plenty of interest.

TOTAL TRANQUILITY

If you are seeking to create a bathroom that is a haven of tranquility and an oasis of calm, there is no better style than one that is pared down to the bare necessities. With no clutter to distract you from a long hot soak with essential oils and a candle, this is a room that will be guaranteed to refresh and revive.

Central to the idea of a tranquil bathroom is a really comfortable bathtub—if possible, one that is slightly larger than average and maybe, if you are lucky, a freestanding one. An Edwardian roll-top version with claw feet is perfect, although this type of tub is not as easy to find as it used to be. However, some manufacturers make high-quality reproductions that look just as attractive as the originals. An ordinary built-in bath can be made to look more attractive with the addition of an interesting side panel, perhaps made of varnished or painted marine plywood or covered with tiny mosaic tiles.

LEFT Choose plain accessories for a restful scheme.
RIGHT White-on-white tiling creates a a room that is clean, simple, and serene.
BELOW LEFT A massive iroko wood screen separates a bathroom from the master bedroom and acts as a headboard for the bed. The rich tones of the wood offer a warm contrast to the blue mosaic tiles that line the bathing area beyond.
OPPOSITE An expanse of frosted glass creates an ethereal impression that is emphasized by pale colors and clean lines. Fluffy white towels add a cozy, tactile touch.

For an intriguing juxtaposition of old and new, combine a restored antique bathtub or sink with minimal, ultramodern faucets and shower attachments. You could also offset a sleek new sink by setting it against a roughly plastered wall, or hang an old Venetian-glass or wood-framed mirror above a thoroughly modern glass basin. While it is advisable to keep other furnishings to a minimum in a bathroom, if the space is available you may wish to add an antique chest or cabinet for storing towels and toiletries, or a chair or stool on which to place discarded clothes, books, and other items.

Most important of all, choose colors that are muted, subtle, and sophisticated. A single wall painted in turquoise or deep red will look wonderfully effective, as will wooden panelling and one or two pieces of freestanding furniture made from dark wood, but the overall effect should be light and airy, to create as peaceful an atmosphere as you possibly can.

LEFT Antique copper tubs, with their rich color and generous curves, are the ideal focal point for an old-and-new room. RIGHT A series of framed architectural prints create the sort of traditional "print-room" effect more usually seen in a living or dining space. BELOW RIGHT Since they share a similar design style, the varied elements of this bathrroom are brought together to opulent rather than discordant effect. OPPOSITE The lovely antique bath and shower fixture makes a wonderful contrast with the ultramodern tall windows.

OPULENT INDULGENCE

If you want a bathroom that makes a statement—a dramatic space in which you will feel invigorated and inspired—aim to create a high-impact look that combines old and new with imagination and flair, resulting in drop-dead gorgeousness and over-the-top glamour.

The secret to achieving this wow factor is usually to include one extraordinary item—whether it is an unusual bathtub, an impressive mirror, or even an incredible view. Specialists in antique sanitaryware sometimes have amazing old tubs, huge shower heads, and oversized, patterned basins—but these items do not come cheap. A less expensive alternative is to use plain modern fixtures and combine them with strong paint colors and interesting freestanding pieces, such as chairs, side tables, chests, or cabinets.

Another way of making a statement without going to enormous expense is to use colored or patterned tiles to cover the floor or the walls. These could be richly colored Moroccan tiles, delicate mosaics, or antique Victorian examples found at a salvage yard.

Since this bathroom style is intended to be ornate and sumptuous, look for pieces with elaborate, decorative shapes and forms—bring on the gilt, the carving, the rich embellishments. For a unified look, however, keep to a coherent color scheme, and make sure that your furnishings either all date from the same period or show a similar decorative intent.

TOP **This bright and airy city bathroom has a dash of glamour in the shape of a lovely antique giltwood mirror hung above the washbasin.** ABOVE **A large silver-colored mirror, a sleek wall of custom-made** cabinets and sophisticated lighting make this bathroom a luxurious space in which to unwind. RIGHT **Unusual freestanding pieces of furniture can add plenty of personality to a bathroom.** OPPOSITE **Plain walls and flooring provide the perfect backdrop for a large Victorian clawfoot bath, a wrought-iron trolley, and a pretty Venetian-glass mirror, all of which convey a feeling of opulence.**

OPPOSITE **White-painted beams and wooden walls give this bathroom a simple, spare country feel that is emphasized by the large square tub and the floor of terracotta tiles.** LEFT **Old oak beams and painted wooden boards are** appealingly down-to-earth. The tiled sink area adds a dash of color and pattern. BELOW **Old wood and bright stripes are a bold mixture.** The dramatic paintwork draws attention away from the bland modern toilet.

RURAL RETREAT

The country-style bathroom is simple and functional, uncomplicated, and unpretentious, with a leisurely yet slightly utilitarian feel. It offers a welcome retreat from modern life—somewhere to relax and unwind.

Natural materials are at the heart of this look, and the most essential material of all is wood. If you are fortunate enough to have a bathroom with a beamed ceiling, leave the wood bare or paint it white, duck-egg blue, or sunny yellow. Tongue-and-groove paneling introduces a country flavor to any room while providing a durable and practical wall covering, especially when coated with paint specially formulated for bathrooms. Stripped floorboards will also strike the right note, although in a colder climate you might want to introduce warm rag rugs or cotton runners underfoot. Accessories in other unassuming materials, such as enamelled buckets, straw or wicker baskets, and hand-painted ceramic tiles will help create an effect of simple and uncontrived rusticity.

ABOVE **In a newly converted attic bathroom, an antique dressing table and rustic stool are placed below a window to make the most of natural light.**
ABOVE RIGHT **A huge built-in closet covering an entire** wall holds all sorts of bathroom items. The warmth of the wood adds to the cozy atmosphere. OPPOSITE **Natural light enhances the peaceful feel of this country-style bathroom. The runners make it warm underfoot.**

The idea of going back to nature is appealing, but not many of us could survive happily without modern comforts. In a country-style bathroom, it is essential to strike a balance between practicality and prettiness. Choose modern fittings such as reproduction roll-top tubs or chunky faucets that function well while possessing old-fashioned good looks. If chosen carefully, power showers, heated towel rods, and chic lighting all have their place in a rural retreat, making for a bathroom that's enjoyably easy to spend time in—heart-warming, welcoming, and homey.

BATHING SPACES: getting it right

• Old freestanding pieces bring character to a built-in bathroom, but leave plenty of floor area clear to create a spacious, airy feel.

• Cheap white modern sanitaryware is good value. Search secondhand stores and markets for freestanding furniture and pretty accessories that will make an impact against modern fixtures.

• If necessary, you can have old bathtubs re-enameled so that their surfaces are clean, new, and pleasant to bathe in.

• If buying old fixtures, check that all dimensions make the items suitable to take modern plumbing.

• If you want to install a reclaimed cast-iron tub, first make sure your floor is strong enough to support the combined weight of the bath, the water, and a bather.

• Use tiles to unify a scheme. Plain white tiles make an ideal background for opulent antiques, while colored and hand-painted tiles (whether old or new) can be teamed with less exotic modern fixtures to add atmosphere.

the elements

Some antique furniture can appear heavy and dark—hard to fit into a modern home. But using pale cotton or canvas loose covers or cushions, or even simply swathing fabric around a chair, will update a piece and imbue it with an air of lightness and modernity.

FURNITURE

The building blocks of any home, pieces of furniture comes in many guises, and a combination of old and new can be both effective and appealing. You may simply wish to add an antique stool to an otherwise contemporary sitting room, or you may prefer to create an eclectic mix that brings together pieces from different periods in an inspiring way. Whatever your aim, carefully chosen chairs and tables, chests and cupboards can underline connections and contrasts between one era and another.

SEATING

Chairs play an important role in the old-and-new look. From a battered leather club chair to a 21st-century steel one, from a bentwood Thonet chair to a 1950s-style dining chair upholstered in zebra skin, these pieces are frequently cheap and easy to find, while being simple to move around, to re-upholster or cover, or to accessorize with throws or scatter cushions. It is easy to make an antique chair work in a contemporary room, or a new chair in a period setting.

Sometimes it is the clash of cultures that makes mixing old and new particularly interesting, and installing a chair from one period in a home from another period can be a quick and easy way to achieve this effect. In an older house, with paneling, ceiling or wall moldings, brickwork, or exposed beams, you could introduce a very different element in the shape of a Danish mid-20th-century chair, a 1960s plastic stool, or a 21st-century clear acrylic chair. The juxtaposition of the two aesthetics will be striking: setting plastic against rough plasterwork or steel against wood paneling is surprisingly effective. The key to making the look work is to keep other furnishings to a

OPPOSITE, CLOCKWISE FROM LEFT **Lofty glass-paneled doors and a stone floor provide a clean backdrop for a 1970 Rocker chair by Marc Held. A burnished-leather club chair is in harmony with modern stripped floorboards and plain white walls. White cotton cushion covers allow an old cane chair to look at home in a minimalist setting,** despite its traditional style. The fabric sets up a contrast with the armchair's carved wooden detailing. ABOVE LEFT **A capacious antique armchair has been re-upholstered in tweed, adding a spin to a timeless design.** LEFT **The lightness of the wire Bertoia chair makes it a versatile choice—it has minimal impact but great flair.**

minimum and avoid garish or distracting patterns or over-complex forms. Trying too hard will only result in confusion, but allow the pieces to speak for themselves and they will interact with their surroundings in a most positive way.

If your home is modern in style, an antique chair can add a note of old-fashioned comfort, a dash of opulence or an element of sophisticated chic. Leather club chairs, buttoned armchairs upholstered in checks or tweed, Louis-style carved wooden chairs or Victorian cane chairs all have marvellous character and bring a room to life. Such elements will prevent a contemporary home from becoming bland, while lofts that are dominated by materials such as glass and steel frequently benefit

from the addition of an unexpected piece that contrasts with their sleek architectural detailing.

Secondhand stores, auctions and the less expensive antiques dealers are all good sources for old chairs. Sometimes they may be a little battered and tired—this may simply add to their appeal, or you may prefer to have them repaired or given a new coat of paint, stain, or varnish. Often the most unpromising piece can blossom into a beauty when painted the right color. Re-upholstering an old chair also makes a huge difference to its appearance: using a plain, heavy off-white cotton or canvas adds simplicity and allows most pieces to fit into most rooms. Alternatively, you could be more daring and choose a bold "statement" fabric

LEFT **Marco Zanuso's Lady armchair looks remarkably modern despite dating back to 1951. Here, its streamlined shape works well in a light-filled contemporary interior that reveals a passion for mid-20th-century styling.**
RIGHT **An Ernest Race Antelope chair, designed in 1951 for the Festival of Britain, makes a bold statement in a modern home.**

RIGHT Verner
Panton's S chair of
1968 looks positively
futuristic, even in a
modern interior.
BELOW FAR RIGHT
This distinctive chair
by Robin Day has
the simple square
lines and clean-cut
character that would
work well today in a
minimalist setting.

that contrasts with a more traditional shape in an exciting and dynamic way. Slipcovers are a less expensive option.

Bear in mind that old chairs can be found in the most disparate places, from dumpsters to yard sales, from outdoor furniture outlets to architectural antique companies. Department stores can provide straightforward, inexpensive contemporary pieces, or you can go to a specialist for a modern-classic designer chair that blows your bank balance.

An interesting chair, of whatever type or style, can single-handedly create an impressive old-and-new aesthetic that will set the tone for the rest of your scheme.

ABOVE **These old folding church chairs in dark wood have a timeless solidity and dignity. They are guaranteed to add depth and character to any room as well as providing useful addition seating.**
LEFT **In this light, bright room, a mix of seating creates an informal dining area. Although the chairs (and bench) may represent a wide variety of styles, they share a visual coherence—all are simple to the point of being rustic, without any ornamentation.**

RIGHT AND BELOW
Old garden seating
works particularly
well when used
indoors. Repainting
it adds a certain
sophistication, so it
doesn't look too out
of place when seen
next to conventional
furnishings.

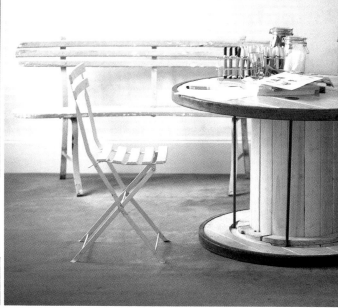

LEFT The rich carving that adorns this ancient chest is in strong contrast to the simply framed modern photographs displayed above it.

RIGHT Former office furniture can often be adapted in an ingenious fashion for home use. Here, the narrow drawers of an old-fashioned wooden architect's chest are useful for storing papers and drawings, and would look good in both a formal and an informal setting.

FAR RIGHT The mix of styles in this home office is unobtrusive because each item of furniture has a pleasing simplicity. The former school lockers are used for the storage of files, computer disks, and so on. The lack of clutter and the clean white floor and walls create an overall effect that is quirky rather than junky.

ARMOIRES, CHESTS,
& OTHER STORAGE

Every home needs plenty of storage, and mixing old and new pieces is a clever way to combine practicality with aesthetic appeal. Whether you are considering a living room or bedroom, a kitchen or bathroom, a hall or a home office, chests, cabinets, hutches, armoires and sideboards, both antique and modern, can play a useful role in daily life, while also making an invaluable contribution to your decorating scheme.

An instant way of adding interest to a modern home is to provide a bold feature in the form of an oversized period storage piece. It may be carved or painted, or possess an imposing, scrolling outline. A Renaissance chest, for example, a

19th-century Italian armoire, an Indian cupboard, a decorative French bureau, a lacquered Oriental cabinet—any of these would create an impact when set against plain painted walls, exposed concrete, bare brickwork, or metal beams. Equally, any of these would provide storage for all sorts of items, from wine glasses to towels, from drinks to office equipment. Statement pieces such as these tend to be inherited (if you are lucky) or found at the grander antique stores and auction houses.

Less imposing (and less expensive) pieces of furniture can also enrich a contemporary room, albeit in a more understated way: for example, country-style hutches, utilitarian filing cabinets, or

LEFT In an airy modern room, the beautiful grain of an old wooden map chest adds character and individuality. Its large top makes a wonderful surface for attractive displays. OPPOSITE, ABOVE LEFT Wall-hung cupboards are a useful way of putting clutter out of sight. Country-style pieces such as this one are relatively easy to find. OPPOSITE, BELOW LEFT Distressed paintwork adds to the character of old wooden pieces. OPPOSITE, RIGHT This mirrored armoire has moved from the bedroom to the living room, where it now serves as an unusual food cabinet.

simple cedar chests can harmonize well with more modern pieces. Such items can sometimes be picked up at house and office clearance sales or in secondhand stores relatively easily, and tend not to be too expensive, particularly if they need some minor renovation in the form of sanding or painting.

In a period home, it is also possible to combine old and new by introducing brand-new storage pieces. Elaborate ceiling moldings, baseboards, and paneling can be offset with plain, pared-down cabinets in wood veneer or metal, their sleek surfaces contrasting quietly with the decorative nature of their surroundings. A modern designer sideboard could easily become the focal point of a Federal dining room, for example, while a minimal Scandinavian chest of

LEFT Dramatic illumination showcases this antique Chinese scholar's desk. Set in a modern brushed-glass screen, it is the focal point of a minimalist loft.

BELOW The color and patina of a painted wall offsets those of the 1960s cabinet in front of it.

BELOW LEFT AND OPPOSITE Retro pieces, especially those dating from the 1950s, have a distinctive style that gives them great character. They tend to be free of paneling, carving, and elaborate outlines, featuring instead tapering legs, plain doors, and a long, low outline that immediately indicates their origin. They offer ideal storage for narrow rooms and small spaces, and frequently provide very convenient surfaces for the display of lamps, vases, bowls, and other objects.

drawers would look at home in a bedroom with a Shaker four-poster. From the most inexpensive chain stores to chic boutiques offering the very latest European designs, keep your eyes open for storage items that would work well in your living home. If designer pieces are out of your price range, bear in mind that some shops have regular end-of-line sales offering substantial discounts, and it is also worth looking for bargains on the internet.

An imaginative approach will reap rewards. After all, at the heart of the old-and-new look is a willingness to embrace experimentation and the unexpected. So, a 1940s polished-steel office filing cabinet would be a quirky place to store shampoo, soap, and other essentials in a bathroom, while a carved wooden armoire could double as a fabulous cocktail cabinet in the living room; a carved oak coffer might hold umbrellas and boots in the hall, or a Tibetan cabinet could conceal a collection of shoes in a spare bedroom. Old pieces can frequently be adapted to modern uses (although

it is unwise to make changes to valuable antiques of any type). If you drill a small hole in the back of an old hutch, for example, you can pass an electric lead through the hole to a socket, transforming the hutch into storage for a television, a DVD player, or a hi-fi system. If necessary, you can even add extra shelving for storing DVDs, videos, or CDs.

Sometimes, no adaptation is required. You can easily make a guest room that doubles as a home office appear more welcoming by concealing files, stationery, or even computer equipment inside an antique wooden armoire or cabinet. Failing that, stack the office paraphernalia on simple shelves, which can then be concealed by an antique curtain or a length of vintage fabric.

LEFT A lovely old oak refectory table is given more impact by its juxtaposition with a set of classic 3107 dining chairs designed by Arne Jacobsen in 1955.

OPPOSITE, ABOVE LEFT A new wooden dining table is surrounded by old-fashioned rush-seated chairs in front of a Victorian fireplace to create a relaxed dining room.

OPPOSITE, ABOVE RIGHT In an almost-empty room, a low modern table offers an ideal surface for a display of antique Oriental artifacts.

OPPOSITE, BELOW This simple old console table, painted white, is an understated piece that goes well with modern side chairs and the pared-down, airy aesthetic of a contemporary living room.

TABLES

One of the most exciting opportunities for unusual juxtapositions of old and new is offered by a dining table and its surrounding chairs. A pleasing effect can be achieved by setting up a contrast between the strength and solidity of a wooden table with a scoured and scrubbed surface and new chairs in smooth plywood, shiny plastic, or sleek steel. Alternatively, combine a chic modern table with old chairs. This look will be even more effective if the chairs don't match, so you can have fun seeking them out in all sorts of places, from yard sales to secondhand stores and even dumpsters.

Side tables, console tables, bedside tables, and, of course, coffee tables can also be essential elements in this type of scheme. An enormous coffee table made from reclaimed railway sleepers or an old Indian door would look fabulous in a minimalist modern living room, for example, while a slim, contemporary console table, made from pale wood, metal, or sandblasted glass, would be a neat addition to a traditional hall.

LIGHTING

If you are looking for just one showstopping piece to bring dramatic contrast to a contemporary room, the answer may be a sparkling chandelier, a spindly 1950s floor lamp, or an oversized 1960s plastic lampshade. Antique lighting makes the perfect accessory to modern furnishings, counterpointing clean lines with ornate or over-the-top details, and cool colors with vivid tones.

THIS PAGE AND OPPOSITE **Antique chandeliers (and contemporary reproductions) possess a unique attention-grabbing appeal. Their sparkly droplets and twining shapes catch the eye and contrast well with minimal modern furnishings and accessories.**

GLAMOROUS

Planning a lighting scheme is crucial when decorating a home, and functional lighting should be installed before any other elements. However, if you want to introduce a dash of glorious glamour in the shape of decorative lighting, then it is best left until last. This means that you can forage around secondhand stores and yard and garage sales, and visit antique dealers until you find the perfect piece to complement your room.

Perhaps the most flamboyant type of glamorous lighting is the antique chandelier, made from wrought metal and faceted glass drops (designed to maximize sparkle) that are either colored or clear. Chandeliers range in style from extremely ornate to relatively simple, and although some cost a fortune, it is still possible to find examples that aren't too expensive. But there are all sorts of alternatives, too, ranging from traditional metal candelabra that can provide a superb contrast to a contemporary living room, to modern, Moorish-style glass lanterns that would look fabulous over a traditional-style dining table. In general, look out for intricate shapes, luxurious materials, and intense colors, and the results won't fail to dazzle and delight.

ABOVE LEFT AND ABOVE The aptly named Fun chandelier, designed in 1964 by Verner Panton, is a deluge of sparkling shells and glittering metal. It would be a sensational focal point in any room. OPPOSITE Nothing is more glamorous than an antique glass chandelier. The larger ones make wonderful centerpieces, and look very striking juxtaposed with contemporary furnishings, while less obvious examples, in the form of wall lights or table lamps, still draw the eye and add sparkle to any living space.

RETRO

Lighting from the period from the 1930s to the 1970s tends to fall into two design styles: the practical and the decorative. The former type will often have adjustable supports or a flexible stem, so that illumination can easily be directed toward an item of study, a book, or a picture, while the latter type comes in wild colors and unusual shapes that delight the eye and create a focal point.

When choosing lighting to work in an old-and-new scheme, ask yourself whether you want a piece that is functional or simply looks good. Either way, there are plenty of styles to choose, from sturdy 1930s desk lights that would look wonderful in a home office to spindly 1950s lamps with conical shades and bold, shapely 1960s lights guaranteed to make an impact wherever they are placed.

Well-known pieces by named designers are very expensive, but it is still possible to find retro examples in smaller antique stores (and often secondhand office equipment outlets) that are highly affordable. And, of course, some retro-style pieces are still being made today —colorful, quirky lava lamps and groovy, sparkly mirror balls, for example, can be bought in chain stores; they will give your home an unabashed injection of dazzling and eye-catching kitsch.

OPPOSITE, ABOVE LEFT The 1962 Arco lamp by the Castiglioni brothers has become an icon of modern design. OPPOSITE, BELOW LEFT This utilitarian desk lamp is useful and attractive in a unassuming way. OPPOSITE, RIGHT An early 1950s Italian floor lamp brings character to a minimalist dining area. ABOVE Disco fever comes to the living room in the form of the ever-popular mirrored ball light. RIGHT A bright-red lava lamp adds a quirky touch to a living room characterized by clean lines and cool neutrals.

TEXTILES

Whether in the bedroom or the living room, textiles help to create an atmosphere of comfort and coziness. Vintage textiles, in particular—in the form of curtains, bedspreads, rugs, pillow covers, tablecloths, throws, and wall-hangings—will add a sense of comfort and charm, making even the most modern and minimalist homes feel warm and welcoming.

THIS PAGE AND OPPOSITE **Liveliness and interest in this plainest of rooms come from the delicately colored and patterned bedspread. The softness of fabric contrasts with the hard surfaces of flooring, furniture, and architectural detailing.**

FLORAL FABRICS

Using old floral fabrics is a quick way to add prettiness, color, and individuality to a modern room. From delicate sprigs to blowzy blooms, there are patterns suitable for any scheme, in soft pastels or more vivid shades.

In living rooms, use old florals to make curtains or upholstery, if you have enough fabric, or make pillows from smaller pieces. In dining rooms, floral fabrics can be used as tablecloths, runners, or napkins, while in bedrooms they work well as pillowcases, bedspreads, or quilts.

CLOCKWISE FROM BOTTOM LEFT **Fabric printed with tiny sprigged flowers on a pale or white background is one of the easiest to use in any room. Floral fabric can be used to cover storage boxes. Seek out lengths of vintage fabric in flea markets and antique stores—you can hang them on a wall or frame them like paintings.** LEFT **Beautiful prints like these, which are taken from archival patterns, are virtually indistinguishable from their antique counterparts.** OPPOSITE **A cozy floral quilt will be the focal point of any bedroom. Quilts look especially good on painted wooden or metal beds.**

UTILITARIAN

In a contemporary home with plain white walls and bare floors, or in a minimal loft full of steel and glass, there is no better way to warm up the space than by adding textiles. Sometimes, however, pretty, chintzy fabrics are not quite appropriate, whereas more practical, utilitarian textiles have the right kind of practical good looks.

The plainest of choices for this type of look is antique linen sheets, washed so many times that they are softer than soft, gorgeous to sleep in or even to use as curtains. Old denim, too, aged by years of use, can be transformed into covers for scatter cushions, seats, or small windows. Thick wool blankets, in muted colors, are warm and welcoming, whether on a bed or thrown over the back of a sofa, and if you can find examples of old knitting or crochet, they will offer the ultimate in homey, traditional comfort.

All sorts of other old fabrics can be adapted in a similar way, whether bought as lengths in an antique store or found in the form of a pair of curtains at a garage sale. Even old dishtowels, shirts, or blankets can be cut up and stitched back together, for a casual look that softens the edges of a modern room. For this type of old-and-new combination, you should use plains, stripes, ginghams, and checks in simple, soft colors—nothing too garish or fussy. But it is possible to create beautiful effects by layering one old fabric on top of another, in harmonizing colors, from pale blue to indigo, or sepia to chocolate, introducing subtle warmth and delicious texture to even the coolest of contemporary environments.

OPPOSITE **Plump pillows and heavy throws in rich jewel colors bring warmth to an understated modern interior. The textiles add a homey air that softens the clean lines and cool neutrals.**

ABOVE **A traditional check gives a new lease of life to a simple chair seat.**
BELOW **These pillow covers have been made from old linen towels. Their soft colors combine beautifully.**

ABSTRACT

To create an interior that makes a strong statement and is more chic than chintz, abstract textiles are ideal. They will work well anywhere in the home—in the bedroom, the living room, a hall, or a dining room; all rooms, in fact, can benefit from their impact and appeal.

In a modern house or apartment, retro fabrics coordinate well with a pared-down, clean-lined feel. Without overwhelming a modern scheme, they can inject a note of color and pattern that provides a pleasant balance or interesting contrast. Fabrics from the 1950s are particularly attractive, with their organic patterns and soft secondary colors. Some examples, such as those designed by Lucienne Day for the 1951 Festival of Britain, are hard to come by and command high prices at auction, but it is possible to find less well-known designs in secondhand stores or yard sales, often in the form of old curtains or dresses that can be made over into pillow covers, napkins, or throws.

There is a wealth of contemporary fabrics available in abstract patterns, in colors that range from neutrals to brights. In a period home they are amazingly effective, counterpointing architectural detailing or antique furniture. Use them as rugs, bedspreads, cushions, or curtains, but use them sparingly, since they can be overwhelming in large quantities. Merely one or two pieces will enrich a space with drama and definition.

TOP AND MIDDLE Modern rugs in 1930s-style abstract patterns add a sleek, graphic element to a period interior with ornate architectural features.
BOTTOM The soft colors of this square-printed tablecloth are redolent of 1950s style, and provide a lovely backdrop for plain modern china.
OPPOSITE For a unique look with plenty of impact, choose a bedcover printed or woven in retro-style abstracts. Well-defined shapes and strong colors such as these are most effective in a room that is in other ways understated.

CERAMICS

Both useful and beautiful, ceramics are the ideal accessory.
Whether sleek and modern or intricate and antique, they add
instant personality and warmth, and come in an infinite variety
of styles and colors. Fashionable modern pottery is made
in strong, simple shapes with one-color glazes, which look great
contrasted with the architectural detailing of a traditional home.
Old ceramics, on the other hand—floral prints, blue-and-white
Delftware, or characterful retro pieces—look particularly effective
in a contemporary setting.

OPPOSITE Chintz-printed tea sets are inexpensive and easy to find. They look very effective when displayed in a clean-lined modern kitchen. LEFT A modern unit has been filled with mismatching but delightfully pretty sets of old crockery and other attractive items of kitchenware. BELOW Traditional blue-and-white china has a timeless quality that allows it to fit into any style of home, old or new.

PRETTY & NOSTALGIC

There is nothing more appealing than a delicate bone-china teacup decorated with a floral pattern in soft pastels. Inexpensive and easy to come by, such old pieces may not be precious antiques, but they have an old-fashioned charm and friendliness of their own. They can be bought in ones and twos and piled up casually as mismatching sets, either to be put into use or simply as an irresistibly pretty display. In a modern home, they make an ideal and unexpected counterpoint to expanses of white-painted wall, wood or stone flooring, and the clean, boxy lines of modern furnishings.

For traditionalists who prefer a simpler look, the alternative is the equally delightful and ever-popular blue-and-white china. Willow-pattern china is probably the most familiar, but any secondhand store is likely have some pieces in blue and white, from all sorts of periods and by a range of manufacturers. Choose individual items and sets for their pretty shapes and coordinated colors, and display them en masse as a fresh, uncontrived addition to a sophisticated contemporary kitchen or dining room.

RETRO

Retro ceramics dating from between the 1920s and the 1970s have a unique style that gives the finishing touch to a characterful modern room scheme. Since they tend to be rather plain, they harmonize well with modern decoration, but they still possess a distinctive character, either in their charmingly organic shapes, incised sgraffito decoration, or unusual colors, which marks them out as a special choice.

While pieces by important Modernist designers such as Keith Murray would be a rare discovery, there are endless examples of less significant but hugely attractive retro ceramics to be found in secondhand stores and yard sales. The key is to pick pieces whose shapes and colors work gracefully together, and to display them in a way that doesn't come across as too cluttered or overpowering.

BELOW AND OPPOSITE, BELOW These simple pieces are by arch-Modernist Keith Murray, and their unadorned forms are typical of his influential 1930s style. They make a marvelous display on a modern wood-and-metal sideboard. OPPOSITE, TOP LEFT Curvy ceramics of the 1950s occupy the shelves in an industrial-style loft. OPPOSITE, TOP CENTER AND RIGHT A 1950s cabinet has become a display area for a set of coffee-colored mosaic ashtrays from the 1960s. The wallpaper framed above them, dating from the 1970s, echoes their colors and shapes.

GLASSWARE

The translucency of glass makes it an ideal decorative element in rooms old or new: subtle and shimmering, it adds elegance and individuality without overpowering other furnishings. Simple forms and subtle colors can be found in glass from all eras, complementing both antique pieces and modern designs. The exceptions are bold, bright pieces from the 1960s, which have an impact and character all their own, and will provide a stunning counterpoint to a room that is otherwise pale and understated.

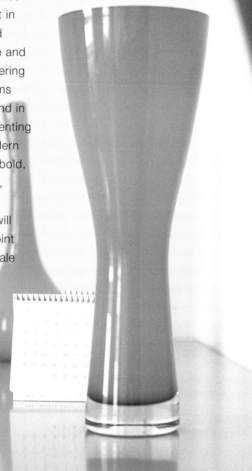

THIS PAGE AND OPPOSITE **These pieces have in common simple silhouettes and lovely soft colors. They stand out best against a white background, and would work in a pared-down period room or a chic modern setting. Their glossy, hard surfaces would also make a fabulous contrast to textured furnishings such as a suede- or velvet-covered sofa, voile curtains, or a shagpile rug.**

THIS PAGE **To look its best, mid-20th-century glass needs a plain backdrop. If the surroundings are too busy or bright, the pieces will lose their impact.**

RIGHT **This modern Italian glass vase has more than a hint of the 1950s in its joyful colors and sinuous curves.**

RIGHT **These vases in smoky shades are typical of the 1970s. In color and form; they make a superb counterpoint to period detailing.**
BELOW RIGHT **These bottle vases are wonderful examples of the sheer vivacity and exuberance of mid-20th-century design. Their clear, jewel shades and simple silhouettes are offset perfectly by plain white surroundings.**

COLORED

Colored glassware comes in many guises. In an otherwise pale, minimal, and understated interior, it offers a wonderful way to add an infusion of vitality, vivacity, and a touch of flamboyance.

Pieces from the 1970s in smoky shades have made a comeback as a fashionable accessory, but can still be found in secondhand stores or flea markets. While subtle in color, their unusual forms stand out against the clean lines of modern furnishings. Similarly, bold 1960s pieces have a powerful impact in a contemporary home, though they make even more of a statement in a period setting.

Glass made on the Italian island of Murano displays gorgeous color combinations and complex patterning. These pieces, rare and expensive, are inevitably a focal point in any interior, and combine well with sophisticated but understated furnishings.

Finally, choose contemporary glass to complement a period home. The right color combinations and simple, flowing lines will resonate quietly in an old-fashioned room.

ABOVE Old wine and water glasses don't have to match—if they are all made from clear glass and feature similar forms and simple patterning, they will still look good together.

ABOVE RIGHT Single items of clear old glass can be used to store other objects such as flatware.

OPPOSITE, LEFT A line-up of antique wine glasses and hurricane vases makes double the impact thanks to the mirror behind.

OPPOSITE, RIGHT ABOVE Salt and pepper pots that recall a 1950s diner make a charming display on a white-painted mantelpiece.

OPPOSITE, RIGHT BELOW These glasses are not particularly subtle, especially when seen with their jaunty swizzle sticks; but they are great fun, and would contrast wittily with a modern interior.

CLEAR

Clear glass can be used in any style of home to create subtle visual pleasure. While it may be quiet and still, clear glass can nevertheless possess strong character and offer delightful decorative qualities.

Clear antique glassware may be shaped in clear, strong lines—a straight-sided water glass or a flowing hurricane lamp, for example. Or it may feature delicate fluting or intricate engraving, either abstract or representational. Each type can bring elegance and eclecticism to an avant-garde home or a simple 21st-century interior. A scheme in which intense colors predominate allows clear glass to provide a graceful counterpoint, while in a room decorated with muted neutrals clear glass is a subtle addition.

Retro-style glass tends to feature more decoration, sometimes in the form of quirky, humorous touches. Such pieces can be picked up in secondhand stores and yard sales—but choose carefully to make sure that what you end up with is not just cheap clutter, but a selection that is both intriguing and interesting.

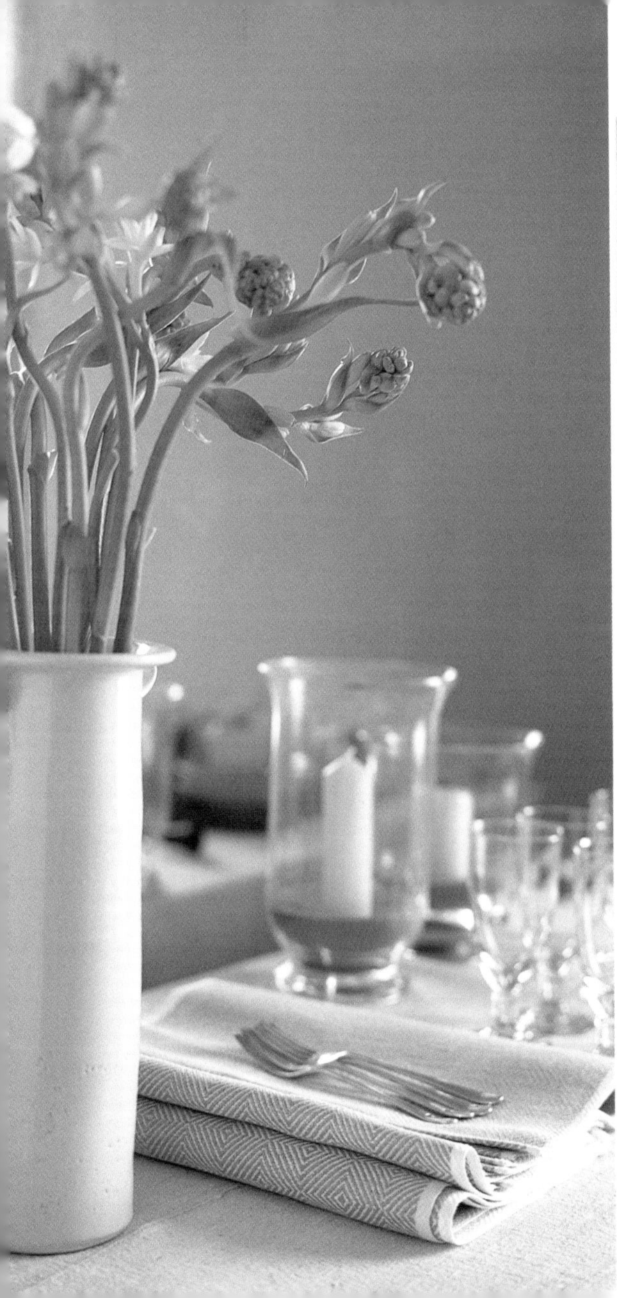

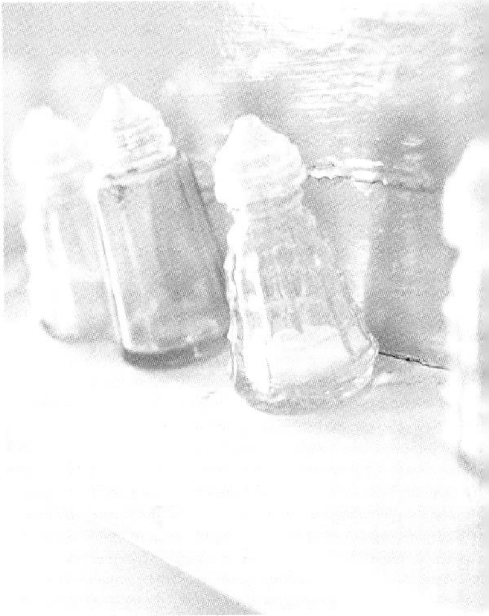

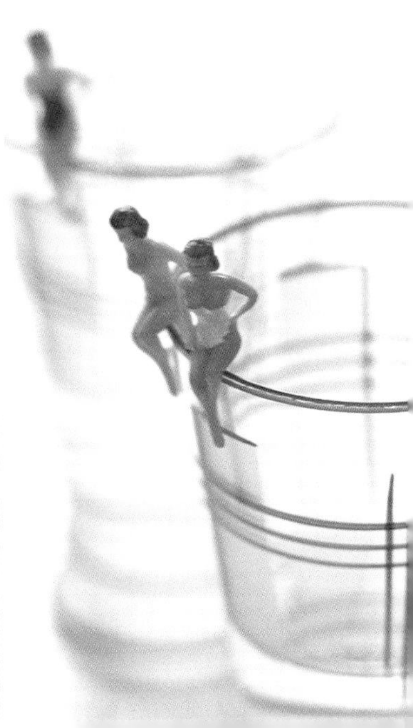

RESOURCES

Many of the stores listed below have outlets in other parts of the U.S. in addition to those given. Call or visit the website to find a store near you or buy online.

MODERN FURNITURE & ACCESSORIES

Anthropologie
375 West Broadway
New York, NY 10012
800-309-2500
www.anthropologie.com
Funky furniture and home furnishings.

B & B Italia USA
150 East 58th Street
New York, NY 10155
800-872-1697
www.bebitalia.it
Modern furniture by Citterio, Pesce, Scarpa, and others.

Cassina USA Inc.
155 East 56th Street
New York, NY 10022
800-770-3568
www.CassinaUSA.com
Reissues of designer classics by Mackintosh, Le Corbusier, Rietveld, Frank Lloyd Wright, and more.

The Conran Shop
Bridgemarket
415 East 59th Street
New York, NY 10022
212-755-9079
www.conranusa.com
Modern home furnishings, kitchenware, tableware, and bathroom accessories.

Crate & Barrel
646 N Michigan Avenue
Chicago, IL 60611
800-996-9960
www.crateandbarrel.com
Good-value furniture and accessories.

Design Within Reach
225 Bush Street, 20th Floor
San Francisco, CA 94104
800-944-2233
www.dwr.com
20th-century design classics.

Domus Design Collection
181 Madison Avenue
New York, NY 10016
212-685-0800
www.ddcnyc.com
Modern designs by Pralo, Mari, Dordoni, and many others.

Full Upright Position
1101 NW Glisan
Portland, OR 97209
800-431-5134
www.fup.com
20th-century classics by Aalto, Eames, Le Corbusier, Mies van der Rohe, and more.

Gansevoort Gallery
72 Gansevoort Street
New York, NY 10014
212-633-0555
www.gansevoortgallery.com
Contemporary pieces in metal, lighting, glass, furniture, wood, and ceramics.

Heywood-Wakefield Company
2300 SW 23rd Street
Miami, FL 33145
305-858-4240
www.heywood-wakefield.com
Modern and vintage pieces and fabric selections.

Ikea
1800 East McConnor Parkway
Schaumburg, IL 60173
800-434-4532
www.ikea.com
Home basics at great prices.

John Widdicomb
560 Fifth Street NW
Grand Rapids
MI 49504-5208
800-847-9433
www.johnwiddicomb.com
Exclusively designed furniture by the original maker.

Knoll
1235 Water Street
East Greenville, PA 18041
877-61-KNOLL
www.knoll.com
Producers of contemporary furniture by modern architects since 1938.

Louis Poulsen Lighting
3260 Meridian Parkway
Fort Lauderdale, FL 33331
954-349-2525
www.louispoulsen.com
Exclusive collection of tabletop, ceiling, table, and floor lighting fixtures.

Modernica
2118 East Seventh Place
Los Angeles, CA 90021
800-665-3839
www.modernica.net
Seating, tables, lighting, and modular shelving from mid-century designers.

MOMA Design Store
44 West 53rd Street
New York, NY 10022
800-447-6662
www.momastore.org
Furniture and accessories by modern designers such as Starck and Vasa.

O Group
(Eva Zeisel Designs)
152 Franklin Street
New York, NY 10013
212-431-5973
www.theorangechicken.com
Deals exclusively in Eva Zeisel's designs.

Pastense
915 Cole Street
Suite 150
San Francisco
CA 94117-4315
415-242-0128
www.pastense.com
Classic diner furnishings, including booths, tables, chairs, and stools.

Pottery Barn
P.O. Box 7044
San Francisco
CA 94120-7044
800-922-9934
www.potterybarn.com
Everything from furniture to decoration details, such as voile curtains, china, pillows, and candlesticks.

Retromodern.com
805 Peachtree Street
Atlanta, GA 30308
877-724-0093
www.retromodern.com
Designs for the home from Alessi, Nono, Kartell, ICF, Knoll, and more.

Vitra Design Museum
204 Pennsylvania Avenue
Suite B
Easton, MD 21601
410-763-7698
www.vitra.com
Designs for the home from Gehry, Thiel, Nelson, Eames, and others.

ANTIQUES & VINTAGE-STYLE PIECES

ABC Carpet & Home
881–888 Broadway
New York, NY 10003
212-674-1144
www.abchome.com
Home furnishings, fabrics, carpets, and design accessories.

American Pottery Exchange
www.the-apx.com
Popular ceramics; includes Lu Ray, Russel Wright, Eva Zeisel, McCoy, Bauer, and many more.

Depot Antique Mall
8313 State Hwy 23
St. Cloud, MN 56301
320-253-6573
www.depot-antique-mall.com
A multi-dealer antique mall in a historic railroad depot.

EBay (internet auctions)
www.ebay.com
Individual sellers; quality and prices vary, with every category of merchandise represented.

English Country Antiques
Snake Hollow Road
Bridgehampton, NY 11932
516-537-0606
Period country furniture in pine, plus decorative blue-and-white china.

Fishs Eddy
889 Broadway
New York, NY 10011
212-420-2090
Overstock supplies of 1950s-style china mugs, plates, bowls, etc.

Kitchen Sink Antiques
North Carolina 27613
www.kitchensinkantiques.com
Specializes in all periods of glassware, dinnerware, kitchenware, restaurant china, and pottery.

Ladybug's Antiques and Collectibles
P.O. Box 574
Crystal City, MO 63019
www.tias.com/stores/lbac/
Selling a selection of glassware and pottery, with an emphasis on American pieces.

Once Upon a Table
Owner: Carol Levison
30 Crofut Street
Pittsfield, MA 01201
413-443-6622
www.onceuponatable.com
European and American period kitchenware; jadeite, Bakelite, FireKing, biscuit bins, and more.

Restoration Hardware
935 Broadway
New York, NY 10010-6009
212-260-9479
www.restorationhardware.com
Not just hardware, but reproduction furnishings and knicknacks for the home.

Ruby Beets Antiques
25 Washington Street
P.O. Box 1174
Sag Harbor, NY 11963
631-899-3275
www.rubybeets.com
Antique painted furniture, old china, and kitchenware.

Tri-State Antique Center
47 West Pike
Canonsburg, PA 15317
724-745-9116
www.tristateantiques.com
Specializes in Heywood-Wakefield, mid-century modern furniture, and pottery, china, and glass.

Up The Creek's
American Antique Furniture Market
120 South Tower
Centralia, WA 98531
360-330-0427
www.amerantfurn.com
American furniture and lighting in Victorian, Eastlake, turn-of-the-century, Mission, Arts and Crafts, Depression, and 1940s Classic Revival periods.

Victor DiPaola Antiques
Long Island, NY
516-488-5868
www.dipaolaantiques.com
Furniture and decorative arts of the 18th and 19th centuries.

www.curioscape.com.
A listing of over 40,000 antiques shops throughout the country.

FLEA MARKETS

Alameda Swap Meet
South Alameda Blvd.
Los Angeles, CA 90021
213-233-2764
Well-known, wide selection; held 7 days a week from 10 a.m. to 7 p.m. all year, 400 vendors.

Aunt Tinker's General Store
Highway 19
Big Spring, MO 63363
573-252-4707
Known for its unusual collectibles, this market is open daily from 10 a.m. to 5 p.m.

Brimfield Antique Show
Route 20
Brimfield, MA 01010
413-245-3436
www.brimfieldshow.com
Renowned as the Outdoor Antiques Capital of the World, this show is held for a week in May, July, and September.

Denver Indoor Antique Market
1212 South Broadway
Denver, CO 80210
303-744-7049
Open seven days a week.

Merriam Lane Flea Market
14th and Merriam Lane
Kansas City, KS 66106
913-677-0833
Open-air market where estates are bought and sold; operates weekly in spring and summer from 7 a.m. to dark.

Ruth's Flea Market
Highway 431
Roanoke, AL 36274
334-864-7328
Over 300 booths selling all types of collectibles, new and old; weekly on Wednesdays and Saturdays.

Sullivan Flea Market
Heights Ravenna Road
5 Miles West of Ravenna Center
Ravenna, MI 49451
616-853-2435
Antiques, collectibles, fresh produce, and consignment; weekly on Mondays from April to the end of October.

Tesuque Pueblo Flea Market
Route 5
Santa Fe, NM 87501
505-660-8948
Native American crafts, rugs, antiques, collectibles, and southwest furniture, both new and used; monthly Friday to Sunday. Call to verify dates.

Traders Village (Houston)
Eldridge Road
Houston, TX 77083
713-890-5500
Largest market on the Texas Gulf coast, with over 800 dealers; Saturday and Sunday, 8 a.m. to 6 p.m., all year.

Vintage Village
I–77 and U.S. Highway
Hamptonville, NC 27020
910-468-8616
New and old collectibles; Fridays 10 a.m to 4 p.m., and Saturdays and Sundays 8 a.m. to 5 p.m.

www.fleamarketguide.com
For listings of flea markets held throughout the country.

PICTURE CREDITS

KEY ph=photographer; a=above, b=below, r=right, l=left, c=center.

1 ph Polly Wreford/Adria Ellis's apartment in New York; **2–3** ph Tom Leighton/Keith Varty & Alan Cleaver's apartment in London, designed by Jonathan Reed (Studio Reed); **4l** ph Polly Wreford/Daniel Jasiak's apartment in Paris; **4r** ph Polly Wreford/ Ann Shore's house in London; **5** ph Polly Wreford/Glenn Carwithen & Sue Miller's house in London, painting by Alan Grimwood; **6** ph Tom Leighton; **8–9** ph Tom Leighton; **10–11** ph Polly Wreford/ Glenn Carwithen & Sue Miller's house in London; **12 & 13b** ph Tom Leighton; **13a** ph Ray Main/client's residence, East Hampton, New York, designed by ZG DESIGN; **14a** ph Polly Wreford/Lena Proudlock's house in Gloucestershire; **14b** ph Chris Everard/ interior designer Ann Boyd's own apartment in London; **15** ph Polly Wreford/The Sawmills Studios; **16–17** ph Tom Leighton; **17** ph Chris Everard/François Muracciole's apartment in Paris; **18** ph Ray Main/ Gisela Garson's house in Stoke Newington, designed by FAT; **18–19** ph Ray Main/David Mellor's home and studio at Hathersage in Derbyshire; **20l** both ph Alan Williams/Katie Bassford King's house in London, designed by Touch Interior Design; **20r** ph Polly Wreford/Clare Nash's house in London; **21** ph Verity Welstead/Lulu Guinness's house in London; **22, 23l & 23ar** ph Andrew Wood/ Norma Holland's house in London; **23br** ph Polly Wreford/Ros Fairman's house in London; **24al** ph Polly Wreford/an apartment in New York, designed by Belmont Freeman Architects; **24–25a** ph Ray Main/Evan Snyderman's house in Brooklyn; **24b** ph Polly Wreford/home of 27.12 Design Ltd, Chelsea, NYC; **26** ph Tom Leighton/interior designer Philip Hooper's own house in East Sussex; **27** ph Ray Main/Thierry Watorek's house near Paris; **28–29** ph Ray Main/ Greville & Sophie Worthington's home in Yorkshire; **30a** both ph Andrew Wood/ Roger & Fay Oates's house in Eastnor, Herefordshire; **30br** ph Catherine Gratwicke/ Intérieurs in New York; **31** ph Catherine Gratwicke/an apartment in Paris, designed by Bruno Tanquerel; **32** ph Polly Wreford; **33al** ph Tom Leighton; **33ar** ph Catherine Gratwicke/Martin Barrell & Amanda Sellers's flat, owners of Maisonette, London; **33bl**

ph Polly Wreford/Kathy Moskal's apartment in New York, designed by Ken Foreman; **33cl & br** ph Tom Leighton; **34ar & br** ph Polly Wreford/an apartment in New York, designed by Belmont Freeman Architects; **34ar** ph Tom Leighton; **34br** ph Catherine Gratwicke/Frances Robinson & Eamonn McMahon's house in London; **35** ph Thomas Stewart/The T House in London, designed by Ian Chee of VX Design; **36** ph James Merrell; **37** ph Andrew Wood/Norma Holland's house in London; **38al** ph Ray Main/Marie-Pierre Morel's house in Paris, designed by François Muracciole; **38bl** ph Chris Everard/Eric De Queker's apartment in Antwerp; **38–39** ph Ray Main/Kenneth Hirst's apartment in New York; **39** ph Polly Wreford/Carol Reid's apartment in Paris; **40l** ph Chris Everard/François Muracciole's apartment in Paris; **40r & 41** ph James Merrell/Christine Walsh & Ian Bartlett's house in London, designed by Jack Ingham of Bookworks; **42** ph Polly Wreford/Ros Fairman's house in London; **43al** ph Alan Williams/interior designer and managing director of the Société Yves Halard, Michelle Halard's own apartment in Paris; **43ar** ph Polly Wreford/The Sawmills Studios; **43bl** ph Chris Everard/François Muracciole's apartment in Paris; **44a** ph Tom Leighton; **44b** ph Tom Leighton/paint Farrow & Ball: floor Mouse's Back floor paint no. 40, cupboards Green Smoke no. 47 and interior Red Fox no. 48, walls and woodwork String no. 8, ceiling Off White no. 3; **45** ph James Merrell/Sally Butler's house in London; **46** ph James Merrell/Ash Sakula's house in London; **47a** ph James Merrell/Stephen Woodhams's house in London, designed in conjunction with Mark Brook Design; **47b** ph James Merrell/John Alexander & Fiona Waterstreet's loft in New York, designed by Lorraine Kirke; **48al** ph Catherine Gratwicke/Lulu Guinness's home in London; **48bl** ph Verity Welstead/ Lulu Guinness's house in London; **48r & 49** ph Catherine Gratwicke/Agnès Emery's house in Brussels: tiles, star light and drawer handles from Emery & Cie; **50** ph Catherine Gratwicke/Etienne & Mary Millner's house in London, ceramics from Selfridges; **51al & bl** ph Catherine Gratwicke; **51r** ph Catherine Gratwicke/The Jeff McKay Inc. advertising

and public relations agency in New York, designed by David Mann & James Corbett; **52** ph Andrew Wood; **53** ph Chris Everard/ an apartment in London, designed by Jo Hagan of USE Architects; **54l & 55l** ph Tom Leighton/a loft in London, designed by Robert Dye Associates, chairs Twentieth Century Design, wooden containers David Wainwright, bamboo plates, bowl and ceramic bowls David Champion; **54r** ph Andrew Wood/Norma Holland's house in London; **55r** ph Andrew Wood/Chelsea loft apartment in New York, designed by The Moderns; **56** ph Polly Wreford/The Sawmills Studios; **57cl** ph James Merrell/John Alexander & Fiona Waterstreet's loft in New York designed by Lorraine Kirke; **57al** ph James Merrell/Ash Sakula's house in London; **57ar** ph Polly Wreford/Glenn Carwithen & Sue Miller's house in London; **57b** both ph Andrew Wood/the home of Gwen Aldridge & Bruce McLucas; **58al** ph Verity Welstead/ Lulu Guinness's house in London; **58ar** ph Andrew Wood/the Pasadena, California, home of Susan D'Avignon; **58bl** ph Ray Main/ Thierry Watorek's house near Paris; **58br** ph Andrew Wood/media executive's house in Los Angeles, architect: Stephen Slan, builder: Ken Duran, furnishings: Russell Simpson, original architect: Carl Maston c.1945; **59** ph Andrew Wood/Norma Holland's house in London; **60–61** ph Alan Williams/Katie Bassford King's house in London, designed by Touch Interior Design; **62** ph Polly Wreford/ Adria Ellis's apartment in New York, painting by Peter Zangrillo; **63al** ph Henry Bourne; **63bl** ph Andrew Wood/John Cheim's apartment in New York; **63r** ph Tom Leighton; **64l** ph Tom Leighton; **64r** ph Polly Wreford/ Lena Proudlock's house in Gloucestershire; **65** ph Polly Wreford/The Sawmills Studios; **66** ph Polly Wreford/Carol Reid's apartment in Paris; **67** ph Tom Leighton; **68a & c** ph Polly Wreford/Ros Fairman's house in London; **68b** ph Catherine Gratwicke; **69** ph Polly Wreford/Mary Foley's house in Connecticut; **70 & 71a** ph Andrew Wood/ media executive's house in Los Angeles, architect: Stephen Slan, builder: Ken Duran, furnishings: Russell Simpson, original architect: Carl Maston c.1945; **71b** ph Andrew Wood/Kurt Bredenbeck's apartment at the Barbican, London; **72** ph Catherine Gratwicke/the brownstone in New York of Bonnie Young, director of global sourcing and inspiration at Donna Karan International; **73** ph Tom Leighton/Keith Varty & Alan Cleaver's apartment in London, designed by Jonathan Reed (Studio Reed); **74** ph Henry Bourne; **75al** ph Alan Williams/the architect Voon Wong's own apartment in London; **75ar** ph Polly Wreford/Ros Fairman's house in London; **75bl** ph Polly Wreford/home of 27.12 Design Ltd, Chelsea, NYC; **75br** ph Andrew Wood/Heidi Kingstone's apartment in London; **76al & br** ph Polly Wreford; **76ar** ph Polly Wreford/Clare Nash's house in London; **76bl** ph Polly Wreford/Ros Fairman's house in London; **77** ph Alan Williams/owner of Gloss, Pascale Bredillet's own apartment in London; **78–79** ph Andrew Wood/Alastair Hendy & John Clinch's apartment in London, designed by Alastair Hendy; **80 & 81al** ph Alan Williams/Katie Bassford King's house in London, designed by Touch Interior Design; **81ar** ph Catherine Gratwicke/Ellis Flyte's house in London; **81br** ph Ray Main/Kirk & Caroline Pickering's house in London, space creation by Square Foot Properties Ltd; **82al & r** ph Andrew Wood/a house in London, designed by Bowles & Linares; **82bl** ph Andrew Wood/Alastair Hendy & John Clinch's apartment in London, designed by Alastair Hendy; **83** ph Polly Wreford/Kathy Moskal's apartment in New York, designed by Ken Foreman; **84** ph Ray Main/Jonathan Leitersdorf's apartment in New York, designed by Jonathan Leitersdorf/Just Design Ltd; **85l** ph Catherine Gratwicke/the brownstone in New York of Bonnie Young, director of global sourcing and inspiration at Donna Karan International; **85ar** ph Chris Everard/an apartment in Milan, designed by Nicoletta Marazza; **85br** ph Chris Everard/ Sera Hersham-Loftus' house in London; **86al** ph Chris Everard/Gentucca Bini's apartment in Milan; **86r** ph Chris Everard/ Lulu Guinness's house in London; **86bl** ph Chris Everard/Florence Buchanan, Steve Harrison & Octavia Spelman's house, Tribeca, New York, designed by Sage Wimer Coombe Architects; **87** ph Polly Wreford/ Ros Fairman's house in London; **88–89** ph Ray Main/Marina & Peter Hill's barn in West Sussex, designed by Marina Hill, Peter James Construction Management, Chichester, The West Sussex Antique Timber Company, Wisborough Green, and Joanna Jefferson Architects; **90** both ph Chris Everard/Mark Kirkley & Harumi

Kaijima's house in Sussex; **91** ph Tom Leighton/Roger & Fay Oates's house in Eastnor, Herefordshire; **92** ph Andrew Wood/a house in London designed by Bowles & Linares; **93al & br** ph Chris Everard/ Sera Hersham-Loftus' house in London; **93ar & bl** ph Chris Everard/ Suzanne Slesin & Michael Steinberg's apartment in New York, design by Jean-Louis Ménard; **94–95** ph Alan Williams/ owner of Gloss, Pascale Bredillet's own apartment in London; **96–97** ph Polly Wreford/Daniel Jasiak's apartment in Paris; **98l** ph Ray Main/Evan Snyderman's house in Brooklyn; **98ar** ph Tom Leighton; **98br** ph Verity Welstead/Alison & Paul Holberton's house in Southwark, London; **99a** ph Andrew Wood/Mary Shaw's Sequana apartment in Paris; **99b** ph James Merrell; **100** ph Andrew Wood/Neil Bingham's house in Blackheath, London, chair from Designer's Guild; **101a** ph Andrew Wood/Ian Chee's apartment in London, chair courtesy of Vitra; **101bl** ph Andrew Wood/Brian Johnson's apartment in London, designed by Johnson Naylor, chairs courtesy of Race Furniture; **101br** ph Tom Leighton/interior designer Philip Hooper's own house in East Sussex; **102–103** all ph Tom Leighton; **104** ph Andrew Wood/Ian Bartlett & Christine Walsh's house in London; **105l** ph Andrew Wood; **105r** ph Tom Leighton; **106** ph Andrew Wood/a house in London, designed by Guy Stansfeld (020 7727 0133); **107al** ph Tom Leighton; **107b** ph Andrew Wood/the London flat of Miles Johnson & Frank Ronan; **107r** ph Andrew Wood; **108a** ph Catherine Gratwicke/Kimball Mayer & Meghan Hughes's apartment in New York, designed by L.A. Morgan; **108bl** ph Polly Wreford/ home of 27.12 Design Ltd, Chelsea, NYC; **108br** ph Polly Wreford/an apartment in New York, designed by Belmont Freeman Architects; **109** ph Catherine Gratwicke/ Sean & Mary Kelly's loft in New York, designed by Steven Learner; **110 &111al** ph Tom Leighton; **111ar** ph Catherine Gratwicke/Johanne Riss's house in Brussels; **111br** ph Tom Leighton/paint Paint Library, chair fabric Livingstone Studio, lamp Valerie Wade, artwork by Zoë Hope, table Josephine Ryan; **112–13** ph Alan Williams/Géraldine Prieur's apartment in Paris, an interior designer fascinated with colour; **114l** both ph Andrew Wood/Phillip Low, New York; **115l** ph Polly Wreford/Ann Shore's house in London; **115ar** ph Polly Wreford; **115br** ph Fritz von der Schulenburg; **116al** ph Andrew Wood;

116bl ph Polly Wreford; **116r & 117a** ph Andrew Wood/Guido Palau's house in north London, designed by Azman Owens Architects; **117b** ph Chris Everard/Reuben Barrett's apartment in London, light from Mathmos; **118–19** ph Andrew Wood/Chelsea loft apartment in New York, designed by The Moderns; **120al, ar & br** all ph Polly Wreford; **120br** ph Verity Welstead; **121** ph Tom Leighton; **122** ph Andrew Wood/Mary Shaw's Sequana apartment in Paris; **123** both ph James Merrell; **124al** ph Andrew Wood/Chelsea loft apartment in New York, designed by The Moderns; **124c** ph Andrew Wood/Jane Collins of Sixty 6 in Marylebone High Street, home in central London; **124b** ph Polly Wreford; **125** ph Andrew Wood/Jo Shane, John Cooper & family, apartment in New York; **126–27** ph Polly Wreford/home of 27.12 Design Ltd, Chelsea, NYC; **128 & 129l** ph Polly Wreford/Clare Nash's house in London; **129br** ph Chris Everard; **130 & 131b** ph Alan Williams/director of design consultants Graven Images, Janice Kirkpatrick's apartment in Glasgow; **131al** ph Catherine Gratwicke/Kari Sigerson's apartment in New York, design by **131ac & ar** ph Tom Leighton; **132** ph Tham Nhu-Tran; **133** ph Polly Wreford; **134** ph Polly Wreford; **135al** ph Polly Wreford/Clare Nash's house in London; **135ar** ph Catherine Gratwicke/ Martin Barrell & Amanda Sellers's flat, owners of Maisonette, London; **135br** ph Tham Nhu-Tran/Ian Chee's house in London; **136l** ph David Brittain; **136r** ph Tom Leighton; **137l** ph Tom Leighton/Roger & Fay Oates's house in Eastnor, Herefordshire; **137b** both ph Tom Leighton.

ACKNOWLEDGMENTS

Publisher's acknowledgments: In addition to the designers, architects, and home owners mentioned above, the publishers would also like to thank Netty Nauta, Aleid Rontgen and Annette Brederode, designers Roxanne Beis and Jean-Bernard Navier, Caroline and Michael Breet, Marilyn Phipps, Shiraz Maneksha, Glen Senk and Brian Johnson of Anthropologie, Tricia Foley, George Laaland at Woolloomooloo Restaurant, Potted Gardens, and Angela Miller & Russell Glover.

Author's acknowledgments: I'd like to thank my family, friends, and colleagues for their constant and unstinting support, advice, and help while I was writing this book.

BUSINESS CREDITS

KEY a=above, b=below, r=right, l=left, c=center.

27.12 Design Ltd
333 Hudson Street, 10th Floor
New York, NY 10014
212-727-8169
www.2712design.com
Pages 24b, 75bl, 108bl, 126–27.

Alastair Hendy
Food writer, art director
and designer
f. + 44-(0)20-7739-6040
Pages 78–79, 82bl.

Ann Boyd Design
Studio 8, Fairbank Studios
Lots Road
London SW10 ONS, UK
+ 44-(0)20-7351-4098
Page 14b.

Ann Shore
(by appointment only)
Story
+ 44-(0)20-7377-0313
Pages 4r, 115l.

Annette Brederode
(by appointment only)
Lynbaansgracht 56d
Amsterdam
The Netherlands
Pages 8–9, 102–103a.

Anthropologie
www.anthropologie.com
Pages 63r, 107bl.

Ash Sakula Architects
24 Rosebery Avenue
London EC1R 4SX, UK
+ 44-(0)20-7837-9735
www.ashsak.com
Pages 46, 57cl.

Azman Associates
(formerly Azman Owens
Architects)
18 Charlotte Road
London EC2A 3PB, UK
+ 44-(0)20-7739-8191
www.azmanarchitects.com
Pages 116r, 117a.

**Belmont Freeman
Architects**
project team: Belmont Freeman
(principal designer), Alane Truitt
Sangho Park
110 West 40th Street
New York, NY 10018
212-382-3311
Pages 24al, 34ar, 34br, 108br.

Bonnie Young
Director of global sourcing
and inspiration at Donna
Karan International
212-228-0832
Pages 72, 85l.

Bowles & Linares
32 Hereford Road
London W2 5AJ, UK
+ 44-(0)20-7229-9886
www.bowlesandlinares.co.uk
Pages 82al, 82r, 92.

Bruno Tanquerel, Artist
2 passage St. Sébastien
75011 Paris, France
+ 33-1-43-57-03-93
Page 31.

Caroline Breet
Caroline's Antiek & Brocante
Nieuweweg 35A
251 LH Laren
The Netherlands
Pages 16–17.

Daniel Jasiak, Designer
12 rue Jean Ferrandi
Paris 75006
France
+ 33-1-45-49-13-56
Pages 4l, 96–97.

David Mann
MR Architecture + Décor
150 West 28th Street, 1102
New York, NY 10001
212-989-9300
mann@mrarch.com
James Corbett can be contacted
through David Mann.
Page 51r.

David Mellor Design
Hathersage
Sheffield S32 1BA, UK
+ 44-(0)1433-650-220
davidmellor@ukonline.co.uk
Pages 18–19.

Ellis Flyte
Fashion designer
f. + 44-(0)20-7431-7560
Page 81ar.

**Emery & Cie and Noir
D'Ivorie**
27 rue de l'Hôpital
Brussels, Belgium
+ 32 2 513 5892
www.emeryetcie.com
Pages 48r, 49.

Eric De Queker
DQ Design In Motion
Koninklijkelaan 44
2600 Bercham
Belgium
Page 38bl.

Farrow & Ball
www.farrow-ball.com
Page 44b.

FAT
Appletree Cottage
116–20 Golden Lane
London EC1Y 0TL, UK
+ 44-(0)20-7251-6735
www.fat.co.uk
Page 18.

Frances Robinson
Detail jewellery designers
and consultants
+ 44-(0)20-7582-9564
Page 34br.

François Muracciole
Architect
54 rue de Montreuil
75011 Paris
France
+ 33-1-43-71-33-03
francois.muracciole@libertysurf.fr
Pages 17, 38al, 40l, 43bl.

Géraldine Prieur
Interior designer
2 Boulevard Pershing
75017 Paris
France
+ 33-6-11-19-42-86
www.geraldineprieur.com
Pages 112, 113.

Gloss
Home accessories
274 Portobello Road
London W10 5TE, UK
+ 44-(0)20-8960-4146
pascale@glossltd.u-net.com
Pages 77, 94–95.

Hirst Pacific
250 Lafayette Street
New York, NY 10012
212-625-3670
www.hirstpacific.com
Pages 38–39.

Intérieurs
114 Wooster Street
New York, NY 10012
Page 30br.

Jack Ingham
Bookworks
34 Ansleigh Place
London W11 4BW, UK
+ 44-(0)20-7792-8310
Pages 40r, 41.

Jean-Louis Ménard
32 boulevard de l'Hôpital
75005 Paris
France
+ 33-43-36-31-74
Pages 93ar, 93l.

Jeff McKay
Advertising and PR agency
203 Lafayette Street
New York, NY 10012
212-771-1770
Page 51r.

Joanna Jefferson Architects
222 Oving Road
Chichester
West Sussex PO19 4EJ, UK
+ 44-(0)1243-532398
jjeffearch@aol.com
Pages 88–89.

Johanne Riss
Stylist, designer and
fashion designer
35 place du Nouveau Marché
aux Graens
1000 Brussels
Belgium
+ 32-2-513-0900
www.johanneriss.com
Page 111ar.

Johnson Naylor
13 Britton Street
London EC1M 5SX, UK
+ 44-(0)20-7490-8885
www.johnsonnaylor.com
Page 101bc.

Just Design
80 5th Avenue
18th Floor
New York, NY 10011
212-243-6544
www.justdesignltd.com
Pages 84, 85bl

Ken Foreman, Architect
105 Duane Street
New York, NY 10007
212-924-4503
Pages 33bl, 83.

L.A. Morgan
Interior designer
P O Box 39
Hadlyme, CT 06439
860-434-0304
Page 108a.

Lena Proudlock
Denim in Style
Drews House
Leighterton
Gloucestershire GL8 8UN, UK
+ 44-(0)1666-890230
www.lenaproudlock.com
Pages 14a, 64r.

Lulu Guinness
3 Ellis Street
London SW1X 9AL, UK
+ 44-(0)20-7823-4828
www.luluguinness.com
Pages 21, 48l, 58ar, 86r.

Maisonette
79 Chamberlayne Road
London NW10 3ND, UK
+ 44-(0)20-8964-8444
www.maisonette.uk.com
Pages 33ar, 135ar.

Mark Brook Design
7 Sunderland Terrace
London W2 5PA, UK
+ 44-(0)20-7221-8106
Page 47a.

Mark Kirkley
Designer & manufacturer
of interior metalwork
+ 44-(0)1424-812613
Page 90a both.

The Moderns
900 Broadway, Suite 903
New York, NY 10003
212-387-8852
www.themoderns.com
Page 55r, 118, 119, 124al.

Nicoletta Marazza
via G Morone 8
20121 Milan
Italy
+ 39-2-7601-4482
Page 85ar.

Philip Hooper
Interior designer
Sibyl Colefax & John Fowler
39 Brook Street
London W1K 4JE, UK
+ 44 (0)20 7493 2231
www.colefax.com
Pages 26, 101br.

Studio Reed
151a Sydney Street
London SW3 6NT, UK
+ 44-(0)20-7565-0066
Pages 2–3, 73.

Robert Dye Associates
68–74 Rochester Place
London NW1 9JX, UK
Pages 54l, 55l.

Roger Oates Design
+ 44-(0)1531-632718
www.rogeroates.co.uk
Pages 30a both, 91, 137l.

Sage and Coombe Architects
205 Hudson Street
Suite 1002
New York, NY 10013
212-226-9600
www.sageandcoombe.com
Page 86bl.

Sean Kelly Gallery
528 West 29th Street
New York, NY 10001
212-239-1181
www.skny.com
Page 109.

Sequana
64 avenue de la Motte Picquet
75015 Paris
France
+ 33-1-45-66-58-40
sequana@wandoo.fr
Pages 99a, 122 all.

Sera Hersham-Loftus
+ 44-(0)20-7467-0799
www.seraoflondon.com
Pages 85b, 93al, 93br.

Stephen Slan AIA
Variations in Architecture
5537 Hollywood Blvd
Los Angeles, CA 90028
323-962-9101
www.viarc.com
Pages 58br, 70, 71a.

Steven Learner Studio
Architecture and interior design
307 7th Avenue
New York, NY 10001
212-741-8583
www.stevenlearnerstudio.com
Page 109.

Square Foot Properties
50 Britton Street
London EC1M 5UP, UK
+ 44-(0)20-7253-2527
Page 81br.

Touch Interior Design
+ 44-(0)20-7498-6409
Pages 20l both, 60, 61, 80, 81al.

USE Architects
Unit 12
47–49 Tudor Road
London E9 7SN, UK
+ 44-(0)20-8986-8111
www.usearchitects.com
Page 53.

Voon Wong & Benson Saw
Unit 27
1 Stannary Street
London SE11 4AD, UK
+ 44-(0)20-7587-0116
www.voon-benson.com
Page 75al.

VX Design & Architecture
vx@vxdesign.com
www.vxdesign.com
Pages 35, 101r, 135ar, 135b.

Woodhams
+ 44-(0)20-7730-3353
www.woodhams.co.uk
Page 47a.

Yves Halard
Interior decoration
27 quai de la Tournelle
75005 Paris
France
+ 33-1-44-07-14-00
Page 43al.

Zina Glazebrook
ZG Design
East Hampton, New York
631-749-5058
www.zgdesign.com
Page 13a.

INDEX

Numbers in italics refer to captions.